COLORED LIGHTS

COLORED LIGHTS

Forty Years of Words and Music, Show Biz,

Collaboration, and All That Jazz

by **John Kander** and **Fred Ebb**

as told to Greg Lawrence

ff **Faber and Faber, Inc.**

An affiliate of Farrar, Straus and Giroux

New York

Faber and Faber, Inc.
An affiliate of Farrar, Straus and Giroux
19 Union Square West, New York 10003

Copyright © 2003 by John Kander, Fred Ebb, and Greg Lawrence
Foreword copyright © 2003 by Harold Prince
Introduction copyright © 2003 by Liza Minnelli
All rights reserved
Distributed in Canada by Penguin Books of Canada Limited
Printed in the United States of America
First edition, 2003

Page 233 constitutes an extension of this copyright page.

Library of Congress Cataloging-in-Publication Data
Kander, John.
    Colored lights : forty years of words and music, show biz,
collaboration, and all that jazz / by John Kander and Fred Ebb
as told to Greg Lawrence.— 1st ed.
        p.   cm.
    ISBN 0-571-21133-X (hardcover : alk. paper)
    1. Kander, John.   2. Ebb, Fred.   3. Composers—United States—
Biography.   4. Librettists—United States—Biography.   I. Ebb, Fred.
II. Lawrence, Greg.   III. Title.

    ML410.K163A3 2003
    782.1'4'0922—dc21

                                                        2003009236

Designed by Jonathan D. Lippincott

www.fsgbooks.com

Contents

Acknowledgments

The authors wish to thank the following people for their encouragement and efforts on behalf of this book: our sensitive editor, Linda Rosenberg, and her good offices at Faber and Faber, our savvy agent Peter Sawyer of the Fifi Oscard Agency, Paul McKibbins, Albert Stephenson, David McKeown, and Tim Pinkney.

Introduction
by Liza Minnelli

I first heard about John Kander and Fred Ebb in 1965. A friend of mine named Carmen Zapata sang a song called "If I Were in Your Shoes, I'd Dance." I loved it and said, "My God, who wrote that song?"

Throughout my life, my favorite poetry always has come from songs and the lyrics that went into them. If I didn't know how to express what I felt as a kid, I could always find a song to express what I was feeling. At that point in my life, when I said, "Who wrote that song?" I had already learned all the Gershwin I could get my hands on and I was also into Rodgers and Hart, Jerome Kern, and Cole Porter. Between their music and their words, those writers gave voice to what I was feeling, and with Kander and Ebb, I heard my feelings stated exactly as I felt them, in the kind of language that I thought was so marvelously straight ahead and in the moment. In that song, "If I Were in Your Shoes, I'd Dance," these two writers caught envy and regret and a lost chance—and yet without self-pity because the feeling was stated in such a positive way and with such passion. *"If I were in your shoes, I'd dance—I would dance on air! I would bless my lucky star, there'd be smiles to spare, if I were who you are."* I understood vividly why the song said what it said and didn't say what it couldn't say. I had found my truth.

After Carmen sang their song, she explained, "There's this

new team called Kander and Ebb. They've just gotten their first Broadway show. It's being directed by George Abbott. Do you want to hear more of their songs?" I said, "Yes, please! Anything else they've written. Anything! And can I meet them? Can I meet them!" A few days later we went to Fred's apartment. I remember it was cold and I had on a red hat with earflaps. The hat was kind of awful but I didn't know what else to do with my hair. Freddy opened the door and said, "Hi." That welcome was the beginning of my career, the beginning of my world, and the beginning of my life as a performer. John and Fred made everything possible. I was like a person in the desert looking for a glass of water and finding a well. They gave voice to everything that I felt, and they still do with every song that they write for me.

At that first meeting, they played two songs from *Flora, the Red Menace*, and I immediately jumped up and said, "Can I learn them? Can I sing them? Can I audition for this show?" At the time I had received good reviews for my first show, *Best Foot Forward*, and I was auditioning for other shows. My agents had wanted me to take a show written by Richard Adler that was based on the movie *Roman Holiday*. I had auditioned for that show and almost had the part but once I heard *Flora, the Red Menace*, I wanted to be Flora. So behind my agents' and everybody else's backs, I kept auditioning for it. They probably got so sick of me, but Freddy and John were on my side. When I finally did get the part, it was a very, very special moment.

Freddy soon became my mentor, my best friend, my inspiration, my guide, and my parent figure because at the time I was a teenager living by myself in New York. There was a door opening for both of us and we walked through it together. It's true that over the years I've occasionally worked with other writers in my performing career, and John and Fred have done so many wonderful shows, too, without me, but we came up together. I paid my dues and they paid theirs, and with *Flora* we got our first break at the same time.

God, in the beginning I had so much to learn and I listened to everything they told me. I often asked Fred how to do things. I'd say, "Show me," and he'd show me by performing their songs. I wouldn't interpret them exactly as he did, but I'm good at taking direction. I'm a director's daughter. I've always said in jest that I thought Fred Ebb invented me, and it's true because there were certain things I didn't know coming from the glamour of Hollywood and a Hollywood family. By his example, he inspired me to become an "entertainer of integrity," that is, a performer who always entertains to the best of his or her ability. Fred was so sure of the integrity he wanted me to have within performing. He knew that I could stand on my own, that I was my own person, and in a way, he later gave me my identity. It's called "Liza with a Z."

Over the years, the three of us worked together on my concert tours, on movies and TV specials, and on their shows *Cabaret*, *Chicago*, *The Act*, and *The Rink*. They became my voice, and I became their voice. You see, I never considered myself a singer. I was always an actress who told a story to the most beautiful music and the most wonderful words I could find. For me to find those two things, lyrics and music, in this wonderful team was so extraordinary. As an actress—and this is something I learned from Charles Aznavour, who was also a great influence on me and who they love too—you find the reason the character is singing the song. You can take a song like "Sing Happy" in *Flora* and really mean it, *Sing me a happy song!* because that's where you're at that night. The next night, so it doesn't become stale, you can turn the tables and sing it with anger, and if you're a thorough and faithful actress, the song still works. It's still powerful, and the lyrics still apply. You can sing it with faith. You can sing it to God—*Please get me out of this!*—with that kind of emphasis. There are many ways to interpret their songs, but of all the songwriters I know, I hear their songs and think, *Yes, that's what I meant. That's what I want to say. And that's how I want to say it.*

Another example is "And the World Goes 'Round" from the movie *New York, New York*. That song can be sung very cynically, or full of hope. I choose to sing it as the truth, that sometimes you're happy and sometimes you're sad, but the world goes 'round. It's that moment of clarity, of humor, of knowing the past is the past, and there's still the future, always the future. They capture exactly how the character feels within a certain set of circumstances at that precise instant, and for me it was the closest to the way I felt. I don't know the precise reasons, but I understood their thinking. I think it must have something to do with accepting one's self, and that's why I've never had to ask, "Should I sing this song differently?"

It's like I've said, as a kid I tried to be quiet so I wouldn't get into trouble, and I didn't know how to say things properly. I felt like the whole world spoke a different language than I did. I hadn't learned it yet, so I couldn't describe what I was feeling. When I finally found out how to make myself understood, it was their songs. If I had trouble finding the words to express myself, Freddy could say them for me, and then the music that went underneath was all the scoring that I'd seen my father use to make you feel what the character feels. After I learned their first few songs, I sang them for my dad. My father was the one who taught me all the songs when I was a kid, and my father was the one who said, "These are the people you should go with. These people."

Years later, when we were working on my show *Stepping Out* at Radio City, I said, "Freddy, I need a song that I can use to show my father's designs. I want to talk about my father." Fred said, "What about 'Seeing Things'?" He sang me some of the lyrics, and then he wrote me a speech that included the line "My father was the dreamer and I was the practical one." Fred told me, "You can illustrate that with pictures of your father's designs, and you can edit them together on film."

That's how we work together. Fred always gives me what I need as a friend and as a performer, and Johnny is the salt of my earth. I could apply the realist and the dreamer idea to Fred and John too. When they're working, sometimes Fred is the one who says, "Now, wait a minute." And sometimes John says, "Now, wait a minute." They may change roles but they get to the same place, which is how to make each piece the best it can possibly be.

I'm reminded that I went to a forum once about my father, and my father was there. He was answering questions for students, and I remember clearly somebody said, "Mr. Minnelli, in *An American in Paris*, when the rich heiress was showing the painting to the young artist, symbolically I think what you were trying to get at was that everyone has their peak in life, and it doesn't matter what area." Then someone else gave another interpretation of that scene in the movie, and someone else gave one, what he thought my father was saying. Finally, somebody said, "Mr. Minnelli, what were you saying? Why did you do that?" And Daddy said, "I thought it was funny." In a way, John and Fred are saying that with their reminiscences in this book. "We did all of that work, but we didn't necessarily know what layers of meaning would be found in our work at the time that we created it." That's what's so great about them—between the sense of humor, the integrity and the talent, and what they bring out in each other, and what they brought out in me, I don't know where to start to tell you about that. You look at the work, and the work speaks for itself. Their songs say what we're really thinking and they expose what lies behind the facade and behind the secrets, behind the bluster and behind everything that society teaches you to be. They challenge and inspire you to stand up for yourself.

How do you talk about Kander and Ebb? They're my heroes. In my case, they locked into the best part of me as a performer, which I think was my humor and my kind of we'll-get-through-this spirit. Their devotion to the work and their respect for each other have enabled their collaboration to last longer than any other lyric and music partnership in the history of Broadway. As friends and collaborators, they kept the integrity of their childhoods and their backgrounds intact—John is from the Midwest and Fred grew up in New York. They complement each other perfectly. They love being with each other, but they also understand working hours and don't necessarily hang out together when they're not working. John loves opera, and Fred loves all kinds of things that John doesn't like. Fred is so into words. He might tell a story to make his point, as he often does with his lyrics.

I remember one time Fred and I were on a plane, and I had been having a romance that had just broken up. I was twenty-two and it seemed like the end of my world. I thought, *That's it, I'll never fall in love again.* I started crying and said, "Freddy, I don't know what to do. I'm funny looking. I say the wrong things. I'll never find anyone who will love me." At first he tried to calm me down, but when he saw that wasn't working, he said, "I have a story to tell you. When I was a boy, we lived in Manhattan near a Nabisco cookie factory. Some of the cookies that they made in the factory would break, and they would take the crumbled cookies and leave them outside. My mom would sometimes pick up a load of the broken cookies in an old pillowcase and bring them home for us. I used to go through that pillowcase and spread the broken cookies out on the oil cloth of our kitchen table. Then I would sort through the broken cookies. One day my mother said to me, 'What are you doing?' I said, 'I'm looking for the whole cookie.' She said, 'You're not going to find a whole cookie. The reason those were in the pillowcase is because they were broken. That's the only reason that we have them.' " Fred said, "All right." But he kept looking. On the plane, he looked at me and said, "But, Liza, one day I found it. As my mother stood at the sink, I held it up and said, 'Look, Ma, the whole cookie!' " And his mother said, "No, I told you, that's impossible." But she turned around and saw it in his hand. Then she said, "Well, you'll never find another one."

"But I had found it," he told me. "And I knew somehow that I could find another one. So, Liza, never stop searching for the whole cookie! Maybe it's in there someplace." When you listen to the songs, and when you hear Kander and Ebb describe how they wrote them and recall the joys of their collaboration, as they do so marvelously in this book, you too will know you have found the whole cookie.

Foreword

by Harold Prince

Until a few years ago John Kander and Fred Ebb were not exactly household names, despite the fact that for almost forty years they have provided the American musical theater with some of its strongest, most durable hits. Songs from their productions are as frequently performed internationally as any created since the golden days of the Gershwins, Jerome Kern, and Richard Rodgers and his two "H" partners, Hart and Hammerstein.

So why didn't the public know their names? That's easy: because they are uncommonly publicity-shy. Because their lives amount to so much more than show business. And, paradoxically, because their work is so accessible (and, yes, quintessentially Broadway show business), they have not inspired cultlike adulation. Too accessible. Too popular.

Reaching back to *Cabaret*, their 1966 Broadway hit, which became an equally successful film, you can discern a pattern. Its title song became one of the most-performed songs on records, in clubs, and on variety shows, leaving behind its original musical theater roots.

Some years later the same phenomenon took place with "New York, New York," lifted from a less successful film to become not just an anthem to our city but an alternative national anthem.

I am told that a whopping 10 percent of the kids in our

schools can't find the United States on a world map. Clearly, if
they were asked what our national anthem was, "New York, New
York" would win hands down.

Though I knew both John and Fred separately, the new Kander and Ebb songwriting team was introduced to me by their
music publisher, Tommy Valando (who, incidentally, also represented Jerry Bock, Sheldon Harnick, and Stephen Sondheim at
one time or another). Apparently, Kander and Ebb (with Tommy's encouragement) had written one musical together, *Golden
Gate*, perhaps as an exercise to see if the collaboration worked. I
either never knew that or have forgotten. I am forgetful, but not
because of my accrued years; I am proud to say I have been forgetting all my life. Anyway, at the time, in my capacity as the producer, I had acquired the rights to Lester Atwell's novel *Love Is
Just around the Corner*. It was a story about young Communists
in our country during the post-Depression period. I brought it to
Kander and Ebb, and they signed on, but not until they had written a few songs on spec. (More of that process will be covered
later in this book.)

That project became *Flora, the Red Menace*, a musical intro-
ducing Liza Minnelli to Broadway and containing an evergreen
score, which still lives, and a leaden book, long deceased.

We followed *Flora* barely a year later with *Cabaret*, and the
fellows began their successful journey. We worked together two
seasons later on *Zorba*, a musical that I believe is the equal of anything they've written. I think bad luck dogged that production,
and perhaps some bad judgment. So, though it has never been as
popular as *Cabaret* or *Kiss of the Spider Woman* or *Chicago*, it is a
masterwork. Its opening number, "Life Is What You Do While
You're Waiting to Die," isn't exactly what audiences paid big
bucks to see. Not exactly escapist. But it is brilliant. And appropriate. Fred and John are stubbornly courageous. They are artists.

John is a serious musician, a composer of operas, film scores,
and symphonic works. Fred is a poet; the best lyricists must be.

Both are voracious readers, infinitely inquisitive, articulate, and responsible citizens. They love to work, but they don't live to work. John and Fred have outside worlds—busy, loving, and private.

On a more personal note, I love working with them. It's fun. I can recall only one occasion when they and I did not get along, when—more accurately—they lost patience with me. Some years after *Zorba*, we opened *Kiss of the Spider Woman* for a summer's run in Toronto with Chita Rivera in the title role. The show was well received and heading to London prior to Broadway. There was only one major problem: Chita's number in the middle of act 1. It was designed to leaven the seriousness of the prison scene surrounding it. It failed.

In July of 1992, I took my family to Venice for a vacation and John and Fred returned to New York to write a new number. Chita soldiered on in Canada, eight performances a week, belting and dancing and dancing and belting this material which never delivered. FedExed tapes came from New York to the Gritti Palace in Venice. I would play them, then fax John and Fred a disappointed reaction. I suppose I didn't bother to cushion my criticisms. But as successive tapes arrived—who remembers how many?—I like to think my replies were increasingly gentle, if weary (subtext: despairing?). Finally, one day in August, I received not a FedEx but a fax from Fred. I wish I had kept it, but I'll paraphrase it:

WHAT THE HELL DO YOU WANT FROM US? YOU'RE IN VENICE PLAYING. WE'RE IN NEW YORK WRITING. COME HOME AND WE'LL GET IT DONE.

So I came home—well, to Toronto, where *Spider Woman* was completing its run. Chita was still performing the number, never once complaining, never once the diva, though God knows she had the right to be.

In one face-to-face session, followed by probably a day's writing, John and Fred came up with a brand-new number entitled "Where You Are." It called for an iconic Dietrich figure, Chita, in white tie and tails singing and dancing with eight prisoners. Rob Marshall choreographed it, giving each of the prisoners canes made of prison bars and slouched fedoras. It was introduced for the London opening, where it stopped the show, as it did for the next three seasons there and in New York. I think it is the highlight of *Spider Woman*'s marvelous score because it makes pure entertainment of the central metaphor which prompted the show.

Think about it: isn't that Kander and Ebb's special gift, to crystallize in words and music the driving metaphor of each of their shows?

In their conversations for this book, John and Fred suggest what I have always known: that there is something incredibly optimistic and youthful about their work. They are not cynical fellows. They have verve and innocence and energy, and I think of these as common to great American theater composing. Read what they have to say as they look back on their collaboration and share the intelligence, craft, and buoyancy of their huge contribution.

Returning to my original observation: if Kander and Ebb were not household names for all those productive years, what really matters is that they are now.

COLORED LIGHTS

ONE

And Then We Wrote

Broadway's longest-running music-and-lyrics team, John Kander and Fred Ebb marked the fortieth anniversary of their collaboration with a series of conversations aimed at chronicling their careers. These discussions took place over the kitchen table in Ebb's home, an elegant retreat on Manhattan's Central Park West where the songwriters have worked during most of their years together. A few blocks away in Kander's brownstone, one of the living room walls displays a piece of memorabilia that aptly defines their enduring relationship. Mounted inside a glass frame is a huge enlargement of a crossword puzzle with one highlighted clue: "Partner of Ebb." The answer circled below the puzzle reads "John Kander."

Fred Ebb, the son of Harry and Anna Evelyn (Gritz) Ebb, was born April 8, 1936, in Manhattan. He graduated from New York University in 1955 and received a master's degree in English literature from Columbia University in 1957. John Kander, the son of Harold and Bernice (Aaron) Kander, was born in Kansas City, Missouri, on March 18, 1927. He graduated from Oberlin College in 1951, and later earned an M.A. at Columbia, where he studied composition with Jack Beeson, Otto Luening, and Douglas Moore.

Kander began his career in 1956 as the pianist for *The Amazing Adele* and *An Evening with Beatrice Lillie*. He later prepared dance arrangements for *Gypsy* and *Irma la Douce*. In 1962 Kander co-wrote *A Family Affair* with James and William Goldman and made his Broadway debut as a composer. That same year Kander met Ebb, who was writing special material for nightclub acts and contributing to revues, including *Vintage 1960*, *Put It in Writing*, and *From A to Z*. Ebb also wrote for the satirical television show *That Was the Week That Was*.

Referring to their songs, Kander says, "I think when we're at our best we sound like one person." But when they reminisce with each other, as they do here, two distinct voices can be heard: Kander, the unflappable Midwesterner, mild-mannered and buoyantly optimistic, and Ebb, the acerbic New Yorker who wears his wit and insecurities on his sleeve. The longevity of their collaboration rests in part on the fact that while the two may often disagree, they have never had a serious fight or falling out since they started working together. Their dialogue is at times like one of their musicals, as either may be prompted to break into song and Kander may dash to the piano at any moment to provide accompaniment. In this first conversation, the songwriters recall the years leading up to their partnership.

● ○ ●

JOHN KANDER: I remember very distinctly the first piece of music I wrote. I was in the second grade, and my teacher, Miss Mathews, asked me a question in arithmetic class that I wasn't able to answer. I was in the back of the room, naturally, and she said, "What are you doing?" I told her, "I'm writing a Christmas carol." She obviously assumed that was a dodge and came over to my desk. There was my Christmas carol, written in large scrawled notes with lyrics about Jesus and the manger. She had me stay after class and she played it on the piano. The school choir later sang it at a Christmas assembly. But I didn't find out until years later that my teacher had called my parents to say, "I just want to tell you that John wrote a Christmas carol. Is that all right? I know that you're Jewish."

I grew up in a Jewish family that had been in Kansas City, Missouri, for a number of generations, so being a Jewish family meant practically nothing except that we knew we were Jewish. We were much less tied to the traditional Jewish neuroses, those famous neuroses that supposedly exist. There were a couple of rabbis in the family, but we only observed on the High Holy Days, and we also celebrated Christmas.

FRED EBB: The impression I have of your family is that they encouraged your interest in music and theater, whereas mine did not.

KANDER: My family was supportive by nature, and I was fortunate in that way. I was born in 1927, and music was an interest that I had from the time I was four. But my whole family loved music. My father loved to sing. He had a big, booming baritone voice, and after dinner we would often gather in the living room. I would play the piano and my father would sing. My brother, Edward, liked to sing, and my aunt played the piano. My mother was tone-deaf, but she had rhythm. After we finished making music, Dad would sometimes say, "Play a march for your mother." Then I would play a march and my mother would get up and march around her chair. Another of my early memories is of my aunt Rheta putting her hands over my hands on the keys. That made a chord, and as a boy, it was about the most thrilling thing that ever happened to me.

Music in our home was just fun. There were no professionals. In those days we made music to entertain ourselves. The kind of encouragement that I received over the years was essentially just to keep making music as long as it was fun. We were never very achievement-oriented, and I was never pushed into having a career. I didn't have any great drive to become a professional musician. Thinking as a Midwesterner, I would say that for my parents' generation, music as family entertainment in the home was a perfectly normal activity, and in our home it flourished. Many homes had pianos. Radio existed when I was boy but certainly not television, and recordings were expensive.

I grew up at a time when even among people who were not artistically inclined there was a healthy respect for the arts and a belief shared by everyone in my family that if you were going to be a whole personality, music and theater were activities that you enjoyed. There were music-appreciation classes and concerts, but there was also a thoughtfulness about what art meant and how it enriched people's lives. The Philharmonic gave a series of children's concerts that we went to, and this was Kansas City in the thirties, not New York. My father and my grandparents had a certain knowledge that came to them through their schooling of what theater was, what opera was, not that they were heavy thinkers about any of this. Music and theater were simply a part of their world. I think those cultural differences in our backgrounds affect the two of us more than anything else.

EBB: Growing up Jewish and lower middle class in New York City, I never had a hint of that kind of culture. As a boy, I had very little exposure to the arts. I would not have known what Philharmonic meant. I had no idea what an opera or a concert hall looked like until much later in life.

KANDER: My mother's father had a poultry- and egg-processing business, and my father worked for him. They had plants in several places in Missouri and Kansas, and my brother and I often drove with my father to visit them. My father's entire emphasis, the joy of his life, was his family. He adored my mother and loved his kids and also loved to have a good time. My parents had a passionate relationship up until the day my father died in 1949, and they were both people who believed that you ought to try to be happy and make the best of any situation you encountered. They passed that down to their two sons. My brother and I are extremely close. Edward is three and a half years older and loves theater and music but has no particular talents in that direction. I've felt a little guilty at times having established my life in the theater, but he's been very gracious about my career. When we would go to the theater together as boys, my parents would be sitting between us and the lights would go down and instinctively we would lean forward and look at each other.

EBB: That's right out of Norman Rockwell.

KANDER: It may be a cliché, but it was true.

EBB: Oh, I'm envious of all of that. I have nothing like that in my life. Looking back, I can honestly say I don't believe my mother and father ever touched each other in my presence. I never saw them kiss or embrace. He worked in a store on East Broadway selling clothes on the installment plan. When he came home, he would sit down with a newspaper and pay no attention to my mother until he was called for dinner. They stayed together with their children as their only common interest, me and my two sisters, Norma and Estelle, who were both more than ten years older than I was. I never saw my father pick up a book. He had no interest whatsoever in anything that would have interested me. I don't mean to judge. He did the best he could, as hardworking as he was.

I remember that he entered me in some talent contests in Atlantic City. I know I was little and I guess I was sort of cute. I would stand on a table and sing "Shuffle Off to Buffalo." I always won the twenty-five dollars and my father would take the money from me. That was the end of that. I remember one night the door opened and two cops were standing there with my father. He had been in an automobile accident on the Queensborough Bridge. All the women in the family were screaming and yelling, "Poor Pop!" He walked in, and I think it all confounded him. I was just a little bitty thing, but I remember the blood on his face and the two cops bringing him in. I guess if I were in analysis I would tell that story pretty quick. He was only fifty-two when he died, or was it fifty-four? I think more than anything else his business finally killed him.

Neither my father nor anyone else in my family had any inclination toward music or theater. My interest came about from listening to recordings that I would play and play until they turned white. I was always bewildered by the prospect of what would become of me, and because my family was Jewish, that was always a prominent question. What would become of a boy later in life when he has to make a living and support a family? As an adolescent, I felt enormous pressure because of that family concern about my future, and I remember that I was unhappy from that time on. I didn't want to be anything my parents had in mind for me, like being a lawyer or doctor. The theater eventually became my escape. I always lived in a fantasy world as a boy, and my fantasy life started to center itself in the theater when I was old enough to appreciate it in my early teens. I felt such joy sitting there in the darkness of the theater, watching the magic onstage. It was such a liberating release for me.

I saved money for Broadway shows and bought standing room, which was fifty-five cents in those days. Sometimes I would go to the theater and ask the concessionaire if he needed help checking coats or selling orange drink during intermission. That's how I managed to see *The Glass Menagerie*, which was one of the first shows I saw back in the forties. Eddie Dowling directed it and played the son. Julie Hayden, Anthony Ross, and Laurette Taylor were also in it. I thought it was spectacular. Laurette Taylor played the mother, and she killed me. I went back many times and I loved every performance. She had a piece of business where she turned around and walked upstage, and as she walked, she reached behind her and pulled her girdle down. I thought, *Oh my God, how amazing that is!* It may have been something that she improvised, but she did it every night, and I wanted to see her play that part every night of my life. I wanted to live in the theater and see every show there was.

KANDER: My interest in music happened earlier, before I could have had much sense about my life other than where the lights came through the window. But I could hear music in a way. There may be some physiological aspect of this, but I think in terms of becoming a musician, much of the process depends on how you hear and organize sound in your head. From the time I was about six months old until just before my first birthday, I had tuberculosis and had to be isolated. Of course, a child with tuberculosis was quarantined, and I was kept on a sleeping porch. People would come to the door with masks on, and whoever was taking care of me always wore a mask. My earliest memory was hearing the sound of footsteps and voices coming toward me or going away. With that experience, organized sound became very important to me, and I can't help but believe that it affected the way I organized sound later on in life.

EBB: Jesus, a sleeping porch. I wouldn't even have known what that was. I never even knew anyone who lived in a *house*.

KANDER: I remember the first professional musical I ever saw was *Pins and Needles*, a show about the International Garment Workers Union. I loved it, but before that I had been exposed to music and theater in other ways. The Met radio broadcasts on Saturday afternoons were a great influence on me. I tried to imagine what the stage looked like and how they presented the stories. One of the earliest experiences I had with opera was a tattered old company called the San Carlo Opera. They came through Kansas City when I was nine, and they did *Aida*. My mother took me and we sat in the first row. There were these giants on the stage, and my feet were dangling over my seat. It was overwhelming for me, even though I could see the strings that held the beards on the Egyptian soldiers.

The next day they were doing *Madama Butterfly*, and I made a pest of myself because I wanted to see that as well. My poor mother, who really couldn't hear music, tried to get out of taking me. She said, "No, you wouldn't like that one. It's not very good." But my aunt offered to take me. So we went to see *Madama Butterfly*, and I came home and never believed a word my mother said about music after that. I don't know how to say this without sounding slightly pretentious, but it was big theater. It wasn't just about music, it was about theater. Years later when I saw the company again and realized what I had seen as a boy, I was much less impressed. But my interest in telling a story through music in many ways derived from early experiences like those.

EBB: On my fifteenth birthday, I told my family, "I would like to see a musical." They hated the idea, and I remember the looks on their faces: "Oh God, *that's* what he wants!" But they took me. I saw Nancy Walker in a show called *Barefoot Boy with Cheek*. That might have been the first musical I ever saw. My sisters and I sat in the second balcony. I thought the show was just marvelous, and they hated it. I remember Nancy Walker, though little else about that show. Years later I had dinner with Nancy Walker and her husband, David Craig. It was one of those moments in life like that film technique where you zoom in on someone and then zoom out again. I remember looking at Nancy Walker that night and thinking, *My God, when I was fifteen, you were the star on the stage, and now here we are having spaghetti together.*

KANDER: When I was twelve, my father's business had prospered enough that during spring vacations my folks started taking us to New York. We talked about making that trip all year long. I had also started a record collection. Records were all I ever wanted for birthday and Christmas gifts. The great record store in New York City, the Gramophone Shop, had a supplemental catalog that they sent out, and I would make a list of records that I wanted from it. I would save all year and when we visited New York, I would browse that shop. We always went to the theater. Coming to New York was something I was already romantic about. When my brother and I came here the first time, he had his head out one side of the taxi and I had mine out the other. Of course, the two of us were thrilled by everything we saw. I remember once we had tickets to *Carousel* and flew on ahead of my parents to make sure that we arrived on time for the show. We had heard the record and we knew the score.

EBB: When I went to the theater at that age, there was nothing that I didn't like. I had no critical faculty whatsoever. But now that we are older we see shows in an entirely different way, don't we? We break them down into whether we liked the lyrics and whether any other elements impressed us. And we're actually able to say, "I didn't like that."

KANDER: I don't go to the theater to find out what I think about it. I'm a true member of my family—I go to have a good time. If I don't have a good time, maybe later I will talk about it. Seeing a show now may not be exactly the way it was for me when I was a kid, but I still go to the theater expecting to have a good time.

EBB: I used to go to find out how they did it. One musical that made an enormous impression on me was *Guys and Dolls*, because I could not figure out how they did it. How did all those elements come together? How do you write a song that pays off later? How can you stop and do a whole song that has no real import in the piece? It was like going to a classroom when I went to the theater. I loved *The King and I* more than any of their other musicals because of all those subtle moments in it. In "Shall We Dance," when the King gets up and finally puts his hand on her, I thought that was the most amazing moment in every way. Who thought of that? The actor? The director? Was it written down?

To this day, that moment is a wonder to me. I gasped when he put his hand on her.

KANDER: I have a hand memory like that with Rodgers and Hammerstein. It was the end of *South Pacific* when I first saw it. Emile de Becque comes back, and Nellie Forbush is sitting at the table. She thinks he's dead and is taking care of the children. She is at the table when he comes in, and they look at each other and they don't say a word. He sits at the other end of the table.

EBB: And they touch hands.

KANDER: They touch hands right underneath the table! Even talking about it will make me cry.

EBB: What interests me always is who thought of that.

KANDER: If you want to think of it professionally, obviously, what could happen when he comes back is that he would stand and they would have a big love duet. That would end the show. But to realize that that single gesture was more powerful than anything you could write for them!

EBB: Yes, but still, who thought of it?

KANDER: Somebody smart.

EBB: And how!

KANDER: Just to get off writing for one second, in *Pelléas et Mélisande*, in the final scene of the fourth act with the two of them, their passion builds up for each other and they've never spoken, and the orchestra is building and building, and he says, *"Je t'aime."* And she says, *"Je t'aime aussi."* Any other composer would have made a big orchestra deal out of it, but what Debussy did was cut out the orchestra altogether. He has just those words and nothing else. Those two lines are more powerful than anything else he could have written, just like the hands.

EBB: That's how we learn, I suppose.

KANDER: I only learn in retrospect. I don't think about those things at the time.

EBB: When did you first take piano lessons?

KANDER: My first piano teacher was an eccentric woman named Lucy Parrot. I started with her when I was six after I had already been playing on my own for two years. I loved her name, and she actually looked like a parrot. She lived with her senile mother in a rather dark house about four blocks away. Miss Parrot was a kind of Wicked Witch of the West. I was a bit intimidated by her and in awe of her at the same time. She was actually quite a good teacher and introduced me to a lot of music that I would not otherwise have heard. She was stern, but on a good day if I did especially well, she would give me cookies and goat's milk—

EBB: My God, a sleeping porch and goat's milk. What a privileged childhood.

KANDER: And Miss Parrot's mother and I would listen to sections of *Tristan and Isolde*. I was enthralled listening to that music and that experience began my lifelong love affair with Wagner. About once a month Miss Parrot would have her students give little recitals at her house. While I was in high school, I studied at the conservatory in Kansas City and played at recitals, but I hated that because performing was so terrifying to me. I remember one time I had to make up the last couple of pages of Rachmaninoff's E-flat Major Prelude because I'd forgotten, and I decided that I would rather be dead than be in that position again. But I continued studying music and performing in college. What was your first piece of writing, one of those funny limericks?

EBB: Maybe.

KANDER: Go on. Recite one. I know you're dying to. What was that one about the telephone booth?

EBB: I don't remember.

A wildly obstreperous youth
Got locked in a telephone booth

When hit by the fever
He screwed the receiver
And knocked up a girl in Duluth.

    I had an English teacher at New York University named Miss
Fergus, who heard that and encouraged me, saying, "You know,
Fred, you put yourself down all the time but you have a talent.
You ought to consider being a writer." Good old Miss Fergus. I
liked to rhyme and later I wrote short stories. I once went to a
short-story seminar at NYU and that's when I fell in love with the
idea of writing. Although I had no formal training in drama, by
the time I finished college I wanted so much to be in the theater,
and I figured the only real chance for me to enter that world was
to write lyrics.
    I remember writing my first lyric about five years before we
met. I wrote it on the bus on the way to endear myself to a composer who I hoped would write with me because I wanted to be
a lyric writer. A girl named Patsy Vamos who I had dated in college told me about this fellow she knew who was a professional
named Phil Springer. Patsy arranged for me to meet Phil so he
could ascertain whether or not I had any gift. He was way over
on the East Side, and I was on the West. I got on a bus and I
thought, *How am I going to show this guy something?* So I scribbled
this lyric out on a couple of matchbooks. It was called "Four-
Eyes."
    KANDER: Go ahead and recite it. I know you're dying to.
    EBB: [*laughing*]

More and more as each day passes
My romance in horn-rimmed glasses
Seems to mean much more and more to me.
Less and less am I concerned by
All the woman he's been spurned by,
Just because he finds it hard to see.

He hasn't got a lot I know
And yet he'll always be my darling, myopic Romeo.
So let him fall and let him blunder,
He remains my cockeyed wonder,
Still the one most wonderful to see,
And how I pray for the day
That my four eyes
Has eyes for me.

Ask me how come I remember the whole thing. No, don't. I'm already deeply ashamed of myself. But that was my bus composition. When I met Phil, I gave him the matchbooks, and he couldn't make heads or tails out of it. He didn't seem particularly impressed, but at least it was a way for me to start a conversation to see if I had any talent or not. Later, Phil sat down at the piano and played a tune he had written. I sat behind him with a pad and pencil and scribbled out a lyric. When I finished the song, I put it in front of him and he played it. That one was called "I Never Loved Him Anyhow." Phil said he thought that I had talent and wanted us to work together every day from nine to five, like regular business hours. He promised to teach me everything he knew. At the time I was working as a credit authorizer on the graveyard shift at Ludwig, Bauman & Spears, but I soon quit my job and started to work with Phil every day. He took "I Never Loved Him Anyhow" to a music publisher who accepted the song, and before the end of the year, Carmen McRae had recorded it. Of course, I was thrilled, though I think we only made about eighty dollars.

KANDER: Why don't you recite it. You know you're dying to.

EBB: No.

KANDER: When I was in graduate school, the head of Columbia University's music department was Douglas Moore, and he became a father figure to me. Back then I was still undecided as far as my direction and goals were concerned. I didn't yet have a specific vision of where I was going. I had written music for shows in college, and I was also writing some fairly dreadful chamber music. Douglas made it acceptable for me to go into musical theater by telling me that was what he would have done if he could have started his career over. His saying that was a blessing, and at some point in the early fifties I made the decision to devote myself to musical theater. I made a living coaching singers, playing auditions, and conducting in summer stock.

I happened to go to the opening night of *West Side Story* in Philadelphia in 1957 and afterwards there was a party at what was then called the Variety Club. There was a large bar in the center of the club and it was crowded, about five or six deep. I'm a very nonaggressive person, and I could not get a drink. But a short bald man standing in front of me saw my distress and said, "Why don't you tell me what you want to order, and when I get mine, I'll get yours." He did, and then we struck up a conversation. His name was Joe Lewis, and he was a pianist with the company, playing in the pit. Later, we kept up a correspondence, and when the time came for him to take his vacation, he asked me if I would like to sub for him. I said, "Sure!" I learned to say yes whenever I could back then.

Joe sent me the music, and for several weeks I played in the pit for *West Side Story*. During that time, they were putting in some replacements and doing auditions, and I had to play for those and for rehearsals. Ruth Mitchell was the stage manager, and when the time came for the director, Jerry Robbins, to start casting *Gypsy*, Ruth asked me to come along, which I did. I played auditions for weeks and weeks, and Jerry became accustomed to having me around. At the end of the auditions, he asked me, "Hey, would you like to do the dance arrangements on this new show with me?" I said, "You want me to?" He said, "Yeah!" and I said, "Yeah!" That was the entire conversation—it's emblazoned in my memory. From then on, it was a fascinating learning experience, but I'm convinced to this day that if I had been able to order my own drink at the Variety Club, I would never have had a career.

It is a terrific education to work with a great director or choreographer. In *Gypsy*, while we were working on "All I Need Is the Girl," when Tulsa says, "Now we waltz, now the strings come in," as I recall all of that was invented by Jerry Robbins while he was onstage attempting to improvise that scene. The lines of that piece were an edited version of what Jerry ad-libbed. Later, when I was working on *Irma La Douce*, the choreographer, Onna White, said in rehearsal at one point, "Is there anything that we can do with penguins?" Then she turned to me and said, "John, can you give us a little penguin music." That moment led to a penguin ballet. Improvisational experiences like that can be terrifying but they eventually give you a theatrical looseness. You eventually learn how to go with the flow of your collaborators, and you also learn not to be afraid of making a fool of yourself.

E B B : Phil Springer taught me much of what I know about lyrical form, prosody—that is, putting the words to the music naturally so the accent doesn't fall on the wrong syllable—AABA, as opposed to verse chorus. I never knew any of that. I had an instinct but no knowledge or technique. I worked with Phil about a year, and then he was offered a job as an arranger for a music publisher for fifty dollars a week. He needed the money and took the job. That more or less ended our collaboration. Phil went on to write some popular songs like "Moonlight Gambler" and "Santa Baby."

I later wrote some songs for a revue with Norman Martin called "Put It in Writing." The show played in Chicago before coming to New York, and we had three numbers in it. I kept getting calls from the producers about one of the numbers called "What Kind of Life Is That?" because it was stopping the show regularly. The song was based on a remark my mother made to me. I was having dinner with her, and she was reading the *New York Post*. There was a story about Elizabeth Taylor filming *Cleopatra* in Egypt. My mother was clucking away and she put the paper down, saying, "Oh, my God, Elizabeth Taylor—what kind of life is that? The poor girl." My mother overlooked Elizabeth Taylor's wealth and fame and felt sorry for her because she was getting a divorce and having an adulterous relationship. I thought that was a hoot, and Norman and I wrote a comic number set in an Irish bar with three old biddies in their cups, wailing about what kind of life Elizabeth Taylor had. I went to Chicago to see the number, and it was one of the rare times in my life when I felt talented, because that number just blew the roof off the theater. I sat in the theater and burst into tears because the audience was literally cheering. That was a defining moment in my career. I still can feel the pleasure I had watching and the joy of hearing the ovation for that number.

KANDER: Who directed that show?

EBB: Chris Hewitt.

KANDER: I remember there was a great punch line.

EBB: [*singing*]

"They packed up the crew of the Fox studio.
They all went to Egypt, but Nasser said, 'Go.'
They wouldn't let her in,
She's Jewish, you know.
What kind of life is that?"

The word "Jewish" got the reaction.

KANDER: Because Liz Taylor had converted to Judaism.

EBB: Yes, she converted. That song really kept me in show business because I had been thinking maybe this was not the sort of thing I should be doing, which happened every third week. Norman and I wrote another number for that show called "The Revolution Is Late This Year." I had worked at Camp Tamiment and we were kind of political then. I also wrote sketches and one-liners for the TV show *That Was the Week That Was*, which was political satire dealing with current events.

I had also started writing with Paul Klein in the late 1950s. Paul was a sensitive, gifted composer, though he later opted for marriage and children and the waterproofing business. The financial insecurity was too scary for him, whereas I was ready to starve if necessary. But Paul and I did contribute sketches to the Broadway revue *From A to Z*, and we had a few hits. "Little Blue Man" was one, and Eddie Arnold recorded a country song we wrote called "That Do Make It Nice." Jim Lowe recorded a novelty song of ours called "Close the Door."

Paul and I also wrote a book show, *Morning Sun*. I wrote the libretto and lyrics, based on a 1960 story by Mary Deasy. That show led an enchanted life at first. Everyone we spoke to said yes. Bob Fosse said yes as director. Our producer, Martin Tahse, said yes. The star we were after, Patricia Neway (just after her success in Menotti's *The Consul*), said yes, and the Phoenix Theater agreed to give us that prestigious space. But then Tahse had a falling-out with Fosse. I never knew the details but we lost Fosse. I think that Bobby might have given the show the kind of flash it needed. Bobby wanted to do it like a ghost story, and he was probably right in wanting to approach it that way. It eventually opened Off-Broadway in a very tragic, operettalike style. I think the reason the piece didn't work primarily had to do with my libretto, which was too maudlin and heavy-handed. Paul had written some lovely melodies. He is a wonderfully gifted composer, but my libretto screwed it all up. At about the same time, you had done *A Family Affair*, which also didn't work, so early on we were coming to each other fresh from our failures.

KANDER: Hal Prince came in as director on *A Family Affair*, which I had written with the Goldman brothers, William and James. Hal was the person who brought me to Tommy Valando. Tommy was an enterprising music publisher who had a keen interest in the theater. He also represented Jerry Bock and Sheldon Harnick. We may have first met in passing through our agent and friend Dick Seff. But my memory is that you and I were both signed to Tommy, and he said, "I think you two guys should meet each other. I think you would like each other." We finally did meet, and that was in the fifth century. Do you remember it that way?

EBB: I remember you coming to my apartment on Seventy-second Street at Tommy's suggestion. He called me and said, "John Kander is coming over to meet you." I was nervous the way I always am, and you came to the door with a copy of the *Herald Tribune* under your arm. It wasn't like you had brought me roses, but I thought that was rather nice. Then we sat and talked for a while about writing music. I liked you immediately and I had a hunch that you would be good for me. That was in 1962, and there was a musical called *Take Her, She's Mine*. We decided just as an exercise to see whether we liked each other and whether our tastes matched to write the title song, "Take Her, She's Mine."

KANDER: Tommy pushed us to do that. It was almost like an assignment. But we didn't get the show.

EBB: Nobody put the song in the show or played it. I don't think anybody ever heard it. But *we* still know it. I could sing it for you this very minute:

I've known her all her life,
    Take her, she's mine.
A child, a girl, a wife,
    Take her, she's mine.
The day comes when
    The lamb leaves the fold.
It's part of an old design,
    And so I smile and bow,

That's how it must be,
    Take her from me, she's mine.

Not a terribly impressive piece, but that was how we started on that first day together. It was a case of instant communication and instant songs. Our neuroses complemented each other, and because we worked in the same room at the same time, I didn't have to finish a lyric, then hand it over to you to compose it. A short time later we wrote a comic song called "Sara Lee" for my friend Kaye Ballard, about one of our favorite culinary delights. I remember one day when we were first writing, I told you that I had a terrific idea for a piece of special material with a comic premise about a coloring book. We had been writing songs mostly in a humorous vein, and after hearing me out, you said, "I have to tell you something. I think we're writing too much comic material and it's gotten to the point where all you can do is try to think funny. Why don't we treat this new idea of yours seriously and write a ballad instead." Sometimes it seems to me that all the good ballad ideas have been taken. How many ways can you say, "I love you?" But our first romantic ballad was "My Coloring Book":

In case you fancy coloring books,
(And lots of people do),
I've a new one for you.
A most unusual coloring book,
The kind you never see,
Crayons ready?
Very well, begin to color me.

These are the eyes that watched him as he walked away.
Color them grey.
This is the heart that thought he would always be true.

Color it blue.
These are the arms that held him and touched him,
Then lost him somehow.
Color them empty now.
These are the beads I wore until she came between.
Color them green.

This is the room I sleep in and walk in and weep in
And hide in that nobody sees,
Color it lonely, please.
This is the man,
The one I depended upon.
Color him gone.

KANDER: We wrote that song for Kaye Ballard also. She was on Perry Como's television show at the time, and on the way down to the show in the cab, Kaye said, "They will never let me sing this song. But maybe they will let Sandy Stewart do it." Words to that effect. We took the song in, and it happened exactly as she predicted. Sandy Stewart did sing "My Coloring Book" on the show, and to our total incredulity, they received something like twenty thousand calls and messages the next day. I could never get over that.

EBB: I remember that we played the song for Nick Vanoff, who was the producer of the show, and Kaye was there. Her image was basically that of a comedienne, so he wouldn't let her sing a serious number like that. If Kaye had objected and said, "No, I want to sing that song," we would have missed out. I still speak to Kaye about once a week. She was one of the first people who had the credentials to validate me, and she did. She is warm and wise and funny, and I'm crazy for her. In my dictionary, under *loyal friend*, the definition should be Kaye Ballard. We later wrote another serious song for Kaye with the title "Maybe This

Time." The idea was that *maybe this time* she would be able to perform a serious piece like that on TV. Later, Liza Minnelli sang it in her nightclub act. That song later became successful because it was in the movie of *Cabaret*.

KANDER: There were a lot of cover records of "My Coloring Book."

EBB: We heard the morning after Sandy Stewart performed it on the show that Barbra Streisand wanted to record it. Barbra wasn't all that hot then, but she was still a name.

KANDER: Who else recorded it?

EBB: Kitty Kallen and a lot of others.

KANDER: The song was a hit, and I don't think either of us was ever prepared for that.

EBB: It made a lot of noise for us. Our having a hit song weighed heavily with Hal, too, that we were able to say we wrote "My Coloring Book."

KANDER: I think I told you the story how some years later I was in an empty elevator at the top of a building, and Muzak was playing in the elevator. I was alone, and as I came down, I heard this big stringy version of the song, and I thought, *I am going to die*. This means the elevator's going to crash! [*laughing*] Oh, I really believed that.

EBB: Others who recorded it sold more than Barbra. Kitty Kallen's was the biggest seller.

KANDER: Barbra didn't do singles, did she?

EBB: I don't know. It was on her second album.

KANDER: She also recorded "I Don't Care Much" early in our collaboration.

EBB: That song meant nothing at the time, though we kept it in a trunk and ten years later it went into the stage production of *Cabaret* [1987]. We wrote it at a dinner party—

KANDER: At your house. We were showing off about how fast we could write, and we said we can write a song between dessert and coffee. The others cleared the table, and we went to a piano and sat on the piano bench. You said, "Well, what shall we write about?" And I said, "I don't know. I don't care much." Then you said, "Play a waltz," and in fifteen minutes we had written it. I love that song. It was one of those songs that just came out simple and full from the start:

I don't care much. Go or stay.
　　I don't care very much either way.
Hearts grow hard on a windy street.
　　Lips grow cold with the rent to meet.
So if you kiss me, if we touch,
　　Warning's fair, I don't care very much.
Words sound false when your coat's too thin.
　　Feet don't waltz when the roof caves in.
So if you kiss me, if we touch,
　　Warning's fair, I don't care very much.

EBB: Before meeting you, I wrote for people like Tommy Sands, Abby Lane, and Xavier Cugat. One of my early songs was recorded by Judy Garland. It was called "Heartbroken" and was on the Columbia label. I was delighted she recorded the number but at that point Judy wasn't selling many records and it never became a hit. That was an early assignment I did with Phil Springer. The song suited Judy because it had some real belt notes. In light of our later relationship with Liza Minnelli, it seems strange to me now that one of my first professional jobs was writing a song for her mother. I also wrote for Carol Channing, who thought I was hilarious. I once sang her a number that I had written for her called "I Love Roz," and she peed. Carol sat there listening to me and she literally peed in her pants! That song was an impression of Ethel Merman trying not to be jealous of Rosalind Russell for doing the movie of *Gypsy* after Merman had starred in the show. Writing special material like that was something I could do, although I had reservations about that world. When somebody has a club act, they want you to write a special song that only they can sing. They get exclusive performing rights to the piece for the rest of their lives, and they give you two dollars and that's the end of the transaction. But that kind of writing is one way for songwriters to start out and gain some experience.

KANDER: Once we started working together, we both knew that our goal was musical theater, even when we were writing special material or trying to write a pop song. I hadn't thought of it until now, but we were both lucky that we had ways of making income within the framework of what we did. You had that world as a lyricist, and I was a rehearsal pianist. We were never taking waiter jobs.

EBB: I never thought of us as being anything but extraordinarily lucky.

KANDER: The really lucky thing—and I cannot tell you how this happened—is that when we first began to work together we fell into a way of working that allowed us to enjoy what we were doing. We never made an intellectual decision about that. We just fell into a way of writing that was pleasurable. But it was just luck that we established that kind of rapport because if it weren't fun for the two of us we wouldn't be working together. Writing is never really difficult for us even if it takes a long time. We never *don't* have a good time when we're writing. We may write junk, tear it up, and then write it again, but the process of writing is never agonizing or depressing. Even writing badly is fun while we're doing it. Everything afterward is hard as hell. But even when there's trouble out of town and concepts change or songs change, the act of writing is never unpleasant for either of us.

EBB: You never challenged me in any threatening way. There was a safety in being with you that I hadn't often felt with other people, and a lack of desire to ingratiate. I always felt confident in your affection for me, and that was sustaining. I don't remember my ever questioning that or going to sleep worried about whether or not you would like me in the morning. There is a freedom, a total lack of anxiety when we work.

KANDER: Which is surprising because both of us are filled with anxiety about many things in life. We carry on even when we don't get it quite right on a particular piece or we get it entirely wrong. Musically, my crutch is my hands. If we've talked through an idea or if you have a lyrical phrase, I have this idiotic belief or faith that if I put my hands down they will come up with something, whether good or bad. Both of us give ourselves permission to be rotten. We may try something and out comes a quatrain or in comes something from the keyboard, and so what if it's no good? I think that is what we give each other that has prevented us from ever becoming paralyzed. When we go into that room, something gets written. It could be pure shit, but that's acceptable.

EBB: We may get stuck occasionally but neither of us ever suffers from writer's block.

KANDER: I don't know about you but certainly for me, particularly after all these years we have been together, contemplating working with somebody else would be like moving to another country where I didn't speak the language. You've often been sought after—

EBB: I would be terrified. I had an offer some years ago, I think I told you, from Richard Rodgers. It was a show called *Rex*, I think. But I just couldn't do it for those personal reasons.

KANDER: I would think without having been inside your head that your first reaction would have been how flattering, how great this offer is. Then all of the sudden the reality of it would set in.

EBB: That was a nail-biter. I could never have been in the

same room with Richard Rodgers, much less have what I have with you where I have the freedom to say, "What do you think of this?" or "Look at what I've just written." I've always been very secure in our collaboration. That has never been threatened, and when something came along like that offer that might have afforded me another way of expressing myself with somebody else, I was not interested.

KANDER: Other people have approached you over the years to work like that.

EBB: I wrote a couple of pieces with Charles Aznavour, but they were already set. The music was already written and I just lyricized it. Otherwise that would seem like cheating to me. I found in you the ideal companion for what I do lyrically, and I don't know if that exists anywhere else. I can't even imagine what I might be doing if we had not become partners. I might have found a soul mate in Cy Coleman, but I don't think that would have been very likely.

KANDER: The truth is that neither of us ever contemplates doing a real project, a whole piece, with somebody else. Of course, we've each done other kinds of projects on the side in television and movies. But it's like a marriage in which the wife says, "You can go have dinner with this girl but you better not sleep with her."

EBB: The friendship triumphs. I wonder why that seems so incredible to some people. Why would we not want to hang on to that relationship?

KANDER: It seems to me that you're dealing with what is most comfortable in your life. It depends on what your ambitions are.

EBB: I don't understand what could be so troubling that anyone could not go on with a successful collaboration. I'm thinking of Sheldon Harnick and Jerry Bock. They were so great together as a partnership.

KANDER: Jerry and Sheldon were always my idols, and now that they have been separated for so long, perhaps some people tend to forget who they were. I thought their work was breathtaking. *She Loves Me. Fiddler on the Roof.* They inspired me.

EBB: But why would they stop? How terrible could it have been? I don't think anyone really knows. When you hear their work today, it's even more remarkable and you have to ask why either would let the other leave. How could you let a talent like Sheldon leave you? And Jerry is fantastic, so why wouldn't Sheldon have said, "Nobody can write music better than this guy!"

KANDER: What went down between the two of them we may never know, and I wonder if they will ever really know either.

EBB: Sad.

KANDER: I think one of the blessings of our collaboration and one of the reasons we have survived is that our way of working has always precluded conflict. If we're working and you make a suggestion, I really know what you mean, and it's not so difficult to try to put my head there. We're pretty good at switching into each other's territory. If I have an enthusiasm for something or if you have a particular enthusiasm, even if we don't share that inclination, both of us will usually jump in and say, "All right. Let's try this!"

EBB: Or I'll be stuck for a word and you will come up with it. I might write something and you may say, "My God, that's really crappy." If somebody else said that to me, I would feel hurt. But with you I understand what you mean and it's acceptable because I know you have respect for my work and I don't take your criticism as a personal attack. Nobody can talk me out of anything quicker than you. If you say that line or that lyric doesn't seem right to you, I'm off it in a minute and I'll change my direction.

KANDER: There is very little self-examination that goes on

in our work. We're always focused on what we're doing. I don't think there has ever been much conversation between us until now about why we do anything.

EBB: We have known each other so long and never had this conversation. I remember once I saw an interview with Nancy Walker on a television show called *The Hot Seat*. It had a terrific impact on me. The interviewer read her Walter Kerr's analysis of how she performed, and Kerr had called her a "Cassandra." Nancy Walker sat there so bewildered by how the critic characterized her performance style and how he put it into words. She was confounded because she never started out intending to be a Cassandra or thinking of herself that way. I thought of Nancy sitting there and thinking, *Who the hell is Cassandra?* I don't think we started out intending to be anything or with the intention of pursuing a particular style in our work.

KANDER: I have a similar story that I may have told you. It's my favorite story about people who analyze the works of others. Years ago Stanley Kauffman was doing an interview with the director Michelangelo Antonioni for a program of film criticism. Kauffman obviously worshiped Antonioni and said words to that effect: "Tell me, Mr. Antonioni, can you sum up what the body of your work is pointing to? What has your message been in your movies?" Antonioni looked up sort of strangely and said, "Well, what do you think?" At which point a very pleased Stanley Kauffman pulled out a sheaf of papers and proceeded to read his analysis of the work of Antonioni. At the end, quite pleased with himself again, Kauffman turned to Antonioni and asked, "Now do you agree with any of that?" Antonioni looked horrified and said, "No!"

EBB: I think the songs that have become what people think of as Kander and Ebb songs are purely accidental.

KANDER: I wouldn't recognize a Kander and Ebb song if it walked in the room and slapped me in the face. Even after writing as many as we have, I really wouldn't know what a Kander and Ebb song is.

EBB: I don't think I would know either. People sometimes call me and say, "Wow, I heard a wonderful song of yours," and it turns out to be someone else's.

KANDER: Sometimes a writer or composer who I know will call when he's working on a show and say, "I just wrote a real Kander and Ebb song, and I can't wait for you to hear it." Then the person plays it for me and I think, *What? Is that what we sound like?*

EBB: We ask ourselves, "Why is that a Kander and Ebb song?" and we're at a loss. I don't think we consciously do almost anything that people have written about us when they try to characterize our music. They often point out things to us that we never had in mind. There's an element of pretension there that drives me nuts even though they may be very complimentary.

KANDER: I usually have no idea what they're talking about. You can write an article about any playwright or composer and imply that the writer keeps looking for material that exemplifies a certain message, but that may not be the case at all. Steve Sondheim's work has certain attitudes in it that you could identify, but if you asked him about it, I bet he wouldn't know what they were. Steve works the same way everybody else does—he writes about what interests him. In a sense, I'm much more selfish than others may think. Deep down inside, I write to have a good time and to write things that will entertain me.

EBB: I'm more of an exhibitionist than that. I love performing and entertaining people with what we write. But I only sing when you accompany me—except that one time when somebody was running for office and we were asked to perform at a benefit.

KANDER: I can't remember who the candidates were, but I remember the story very well and I still can't believe that you did it.

EBB: It was at the Palace Theater. Samuels. He was my candidate—

KANDER: Howard Samuels. God damn! Let me tell this story because you remember it somewhat differently than I do. You were terribly excited because we had been asked to perform at this rally at the Palace for this gubernatorial candidate, Howard Samuels. But I said, "I'm not for him." And you said, "What difference does it make? It's the Palace!" Fred, if Hitler asked you to perform at the Palace, you would do it. You said yes to playing at the Palace, and I refused to do it.

EBB: I said, "Look at who's performing, Alan J. Lerner and Yip Harburg. And Chita is going to introduce us!" It was kind of swanky. Paul Trueblood accompanied me. I sang "Ring Them Bells" and I killed them. I just didn't see how you could resist walking out onstage at the Palace.

KANDER: I was appalled.

EBB: I told the audience, "Imagine standing here where Sophie Tucker and Al Jolson once stood!" I had never sung before without you.

KANDER: I always hated performing, but you were terrific and people always wanted us to perform because of you.

EBB: I enjoyed those occasional benefits, the one-shot deals. I loved performing. I was very sick for a while, and my voice went. Then I realized I wasn't good anymore. I became nasal and insecure. What you need is confidence, and I lost that. But even recently we received a couple offers to perform professionally.

KANDER: Four little words: "Not on your life." You would have liked to, but I just couldn't do it. I was terrified every time we performed together, mostly that I would forget how to play the piano. It's absolutely true. I've had terrible stage fright ever since college. I was playing a show that I had written at Oberlin. I was all there was in the pit, just me and the piano. Between the matinee and evening performance, I had a drink. It was just one glass of wine, but it did something to my concentration. When I came back and started the show, I began to think, *Why am I pushing down this white thing? What's the next thing my hands are supposed to do?* It was as if I were a dancer and suddenly had to remember what muscles to use to lift my leg. I became totally involved in the mechanics of how the machine worked, and I froze. It was only a second or two, but I never got over it. It wasn't a fear of forgetting how a song goes, it was a fear of forgetting how to make the machine work.

I never lost that stage fright, and that was the reason I stopped performing years ago. Even to this day, I actually think that I'm going to forget how to play the instrument. You and our friend Liza Minnelli used to tease me about that. I remember the three of us once got up and performed a tribute for George Abbott, and the two of you were going like gangbusters. At some point you looked over and saw my eyeballs rolling to the back of my head. During moments like that, I felt that if I took my hands off the keyboard I would never put them back down. You and Liza never teased me about it again after that because you knew it was real.

EBB: I've seen your hands shake.

KANDER: It's never there when we're working or when I'm playing something for myself. I think if you start to think about how you do something, you freeze. If we're working on a scene in a rehearsal and suddenly the director says, "We need some music to get from this point to that point," if I think about it, I can't do it. If I just go to the piano and put my hands down, immediately my fingers will invent. It has nothing to do with my brain. It just happens, but I have to let myself do it. When I watch you working, I don't think of it as an intellectual exercise. I think of it as an oral or verbal process. You get the rhyme scheme worked out, and there is suddenly a quatrain that didn't exist before. It's not because you sit down and think and take notes and examine it. Sometimes that may be true, but most of the time it comes out in this effortless way like what I feel when I put my fingers on the piano.

EBB: I think the reason for that effortlessness is confidence. I feel confident when I've written something that you will properly set it musically and that I will like the song when you're finished. We know how to please each other musically and the collaboration works on the basis of that kind of mutual support, which we agree neither of us would necessarily have if we were to sit in a room and try to write with someone else.

KANDER: I think when we're at our best, we sound like one person. But there's no pride in it. We would be paralyzed if we had someone looking over our shoulder and telling us that what we were writing had to be good. We have finished whole songs and come back the next day and torn them up. Neither of us says, "Oh my God, what am I going to do with my life now that I've written something so terrible?"

EBB: It's back to square one.

KANDER: That was our philosophy from the very beginning.

EBB: When it doesn't work, go back to square one and try again and hope we get lucky this time. *Maybe this time*, get it?

TWO

Flora, the Red Menace

Though not the first show they wrote, *Flora, the Red Menace* was Kander and Ebb's first Broadway musical, a satire of 1930s radicals and Greenwich Village bohemianism. The heroine of the piece was an aspiring fashion designer whose boyfriend convinces her to join the Communist Party. Produced by Harold Prince and directed by George Abbott, the show opened at the Alvin Theater on May 11, 1965. Though it ran for only eighty-seven performances, *Flora* quickly established Kander and Ebb as up-and-coming musical comedy stylists (the cast album spent two months on the charts) and earned nineteen-year-old Liza Minnelli a Tony for her first leading role on Broadway. On the opening night of *Flora*, Liza scored with her second-act number "Sing Happy," foreshadowing what was to come in the years ahead for the songwriters and their favorite muse.

• ● •

EBB: Not long after we first met, Richard Morris showed us a book he had written for a show called *Golden Gate*, and we wrote the score. The libretto was about the rebuilding of San Francisco after the 1906 earthquake.

KANDER: Richard was a friend of yours.

EBB: Kaye Ballard had introduced me to him. I was going to

California and I had no place to stay. She called Richard and arranged for me to stay with him.

KANDER: We knew him before anything had happened to us, and he was part of a whole Hollywood world that I had never seen.

EBB: Richard was very successful. He wrote the *Loretta Young Show* for many years. He also wrote *The Unsinkable Molly Brown* and *Thoroughly Modern Millie.*

KANDER: He knew everybody.

EBB: Yeah, Jan Sterling and Paul Douglas used to hang out with him all the time. Loretta Young came to dinner. Those were the kind of people Richard knew. He impressed the hell out of me.

KANDER: His book for *Golden Gate* was based on a real character who was known as Emperor Norton, and he was a wildly eccentric guy who declared himself the Emperor of San Francisco —

EBB: And all the outer islands.

KANDER: San Francisco, being the kind of city it is, treated him like he was an emperor.

EBB: He lived in the Palace Hotel and was much beloved. Nobody ever charged him when he went to restaurants, and he had a ring and a ball of wax that he used for an official seal. He was out of our 1906 time frame, actually, but we appropriated him. We saw Mickey Rooney playing that role.

KANDER: We were out in California staying with Richard —

EBB: And we played a big backers' audition in San Francisco. I remember a hall filled with people, and we played some of our songs to raise money for this enterprise. But it never happened.

KANDER: We did have a good time working on that score. Shall we tell the shower story?

EBB: Sure.

KANDER: You and Richard gave me an assignment at a certain point, saying, "All we need here is the most passionate, most romantic melody in the world." Then the two of you left me alone. All I could think to do was to play this piece— [*playing piano*]

EBB: I went to take a shower and I heard this glorious melody. I said, "Oh, my God, John!" I rushed out of the shower and told you, "That's the best thing I've ever heard in my life." I actually started to write a lyric for it. What was it?

KANDER: The music was *Turandot*. You were terribly excited, and I said, "Thanks! That's Puccini."

EBB: Oh, I loved that piece. I thought it was the most beautiful thing.

KANDER: We used to play songs for Tommy Valando over the telephone. Tommy was a very theatrical guy. You would sing him pieces that we were writing. I remember we had written one song we were kind of in love with while we were writing, and we played it for him over the phone, expecting a big response. He was a very exuberant person. But there was a long silence, and just as I had done with your reaction to *Turandot*, he said, "Are you kidding!" The lyric was basically from a Duke Ellington song and the melody was a distorted version of a song from *No Strings*. We had both done it and had no idea we had done it. Of course, we never published it.

EBB: Right. "Prelude to a Kiss" was another one where I stole the title.

KANDER: But you do those things and you don't know it consciously.

EBB: I think that's what happened with Jerry Herman. He was sued by Mack David over the song "Hello, Dolly!" But Jerry didn't mean to take any of that material.

KANDER: Nobody intends to do that.

EBB: You get nailed after you've done it.

KANDER: Who was that priest who wrote those musicals? Carmine?

EBB: Al Carmine.

KANDER: He wrote some things that were really quite good, and somebody wrote a review of him saying, "Every piece of music that Carmine has ever heard has gone in one ear and stayed there."

EBB: [*laughing*] He was good, though.

KANDER: *Golden Gate* gave us our first real show.

EBB: We auditioned with that score.

KANDER: That's what landed us *Flora, the Red Menace*.

EBB: We played it for George Abbott. He liked it and I remember him smiling and saying, "That's fine." That experience was unbelievable. Now that I look back on it, it has almost a dreamlike quality. It was amazing just to be in the same room with a legend like Mr. Abbott.

KANDER: Hal Prince was the one who set up the audition.

EBB: You knew Hal from working with him on *A Family Affair*. I did not know Hal as well, and when we used to go to his office for whatever reason, invariably when we were leaving, Hal would say, "Hey, Johnny, come in here." You would go in and I would be left standing in the anteroom or by the elevators. I felt left out of things because the two of you had that relationship. Of course, it wasn't anybody's fault.

KANDER: You felt that way with Mary Rodgers, too?

EBB: Yes, I had a brief association with her, and she and Hal had a way of communicating that excluded me. It used to hurt. But after we played for George Abbott and got the show, I developed more of a relationship with Hal. Later, I traveled to Europe with him and we became friends. But we were offered *Flora* based entirely on our work with *Golden Gate*.

KANDER: Hal had bought the rights to a book called *Love Is Just around the Corner*, which came out during a newspaper strike and was never reviewed.

EBB: Lester Atwell was the author.

KANDER: It was a novel based on his memories of the early

thirties, and the Communist Party and life in New York—a beautiful, funny, touching story. Hal read the galleys and immediately thought of it as a musical. In those days he hadn't really started directing yet. He had directed *A Family Affair* in less than ten days, and that was his first directing experience on Broadway. But he also acquired projects for Mr. Abbott and worked out of his office. They had a very close business relationship for many years. Hal produced the show for Abbott, who was probably the wrong person to direct that show. As wonderful a man as he was, he really didn't have an affinity for the material. Hal later said he wished he had directed it himself.

E B B : Hal asked us to write six songs on spec and play them for him. I think all of them were used in the show except for "The Kid Herself."

K A N D E R : Mr. Abbott was very supportive in his rough way even if he was rejecting things. He would never cut us down to size.

E B B : Hal was also very supportive of us and obviously pushing for us to get this show. The first time we played those six songs, we played them for Hal and his wife, Judy, at their East Side apartment. That gave us confidence because they liked them so much. Then we went on to do it. The experience of working on *Flora* was thrilling, the kind of situation where I wanted to just go off in a corner and cry because I could hardly believe it was really happening, our first Broadway show. I don't remember having any sense of pride or ego. I was always prayerful about the work—I hope they like it, I hope it works, I hope it's as good as it sounds to me—but the truth is you never know.

K A N D E R : In those days we wrote a lot, and we threw away a lot.

E B B : With *Flora* we must have written sixty songs, out of which they chose fifteen.

K A N D E R : That was true for *Cabaret* as well.

EBB: We kept going home and writing.

KANDER: We wrote very fast, and we tore them up very fast. But every once in a while we would write a song we both had affection for. In *Flora*, "A Quiet Thing" was one of them.

EBB: We also knew that they were not going to cut that song. I remember at one point during rehearsals Mr. Abbott wanted a ballad, so Mr. Abbott got a ballad. But as you know, a ballad is the most difficult kind of song for me to write. I never quite know how to begin one. We were envisioning a scene in which Flora gets her big break. You said to me, "Let's approach the moment this way. Did anything ever happen to you in your life like when everything came true, everything you ever dreamed?" I said, "Yes, when we signed to do this show." Then you asked me what I felt at that moment, and I said, "Oh, nothing." I mean there it was, *nothing*, and that is what the song is about. I know without your suggestion I would never have approached the lyrics that way:

When it all comes true
Just the way you planned,
It's funny but the bells don't ring.
It's a quiet thing.
When you hold the world
In your trembling hand,
You'd think you'd hear a choir sing,
It's a quiet thing.

There are no exploding fireworks.
Where's the roaring of the crowds?
Maybe it's this strange new atmosphere
Way up here among the clouds,

But I don't hear the drums,
I don't hear the band,

The sounds I'm told such moments bring.
Happiness comes in on tiptoe,
Well, whatd'ya know?
It's a quiet thing.
A very quiet thing.

KANDER: I'm mushy about this memory. To most people, the idea is that if you get good news you immediately start to jump up and down, but you may not necessarily react that way.

EBB: It's happened again since then. I remember you calling to say, "I have some good news for you. We won the Kennedy Center Honor." I couldn't be anything but quiet. I could have run to the window, opened it, and screamed. But I didn't.

KANDER: But being quiet doesn't mean you're not deeply affected.

EBB: I was totally serene, if you can imagine, and what a high point in life. I don't think I've ever reacted any other way to great news. I've always been quiet about it.

KANDER: I tend to react that way also. I think that what we try to do instinctively is write something that is true. It's really as simple as that. Often when we're writing a moment for a musical, we'll be working on an idea and one of us will say, "She wouldn't talk like that. This character wouldn't say that." I don't think of the way we work as mysterious at all. We try very hard to let the character be true to himself or herself. There will be musical things that are not true. It may seem strange to describe something as abstract as music as being true or false, but there are ways that a melody can be shaped or the rhythmic underpinnings of a song can be written that are simply not true.

EBB: The truth is the character would never sound like that.

KANDER: If you take a Schubert song, and put the microscope to it—to one of his great songs—it's all true, down to the last note and what he does with the prosody.

EBB: Or take a musical comedy song. Take "Adelaide's

Lament" in *Guys and Dolls*. Look at what that woman is saying. "You can spray her wherever the streptococci lurk." You say to yourself, *Would Adelaide say "streptococci"?* Yes, it sounds right and is wonderfully funny. You never heard that word in a song before, and it's a delight. I actually made a noise in the theater when I heard that lyric. Oh, what a song! I would have killed to have written that.

KANDER: You know what's interesting about that lyric, too? Forget the rhyme situation—if Frank Loesser had used the word "streptococcus," it wouldn't be funny. It's the "i" that makes it funny. And if you try to explain why the "i" makes it funny, you can't.

EBB: Getting back to *Flora*, at the time that we were writing the score, there was a girl in New York named Marge Cameron, who is now Carmen Zapata, and I had written some special material for her. Marge was performing with Liza Minnelli in *Carnival* out on Long Island. Marge said, "Oh, you've just got to see Liza; she's wonderful!" Liza apparently had a record deal, so Marge, trying to be helpful, said, "I'd like to bring her over to hear some of the songs you and John have written, and maybe she'll put one on her record." I had no interest in her, but Marge was relentless. Liza eventually came to my apartment to meet us. She was only seventeen. Her hair was long and stringy, and she wore funny-looking clothes, like this red hat with earflaps.

KANDER: She was messy in those days and didn't know how to make herself as attractive as she is. She didn't have what she developed later, that Liza style.

EBB: She sat on the couch, took off her shoes and tucked her legs under her. We played her some songs but didn't get much of a reaction. Then Liza said, "What are you writing now?" We told her we were writing a musical called *Flora, the Red Menace,* and she said, "Can I hear some of those songs?" We played two or three numbers, and Liza suddenly became animated, jumped up, and said, "Can I try singing that?" I remember she stood behind you and read the lyrics over your shoulder. When she began to sing, I was wild for her. I thought, *This girl is terrific!*

KANDER: It was easy to see how talented she was.

EBB: And we had been having trouble finding a Flora. It seemed like the perfect thing for Liza to do. At the time, she had another show that Richard Adler had written, based on the movie *Roman Holiday*. She was going to do that, but then she heard *Flora* and obviously wanted to do it. She was all over the place, saying, "Oh, can I be in it? Who do I have to speak to? Who does my agent have to call?" So we set up an audition. But George Abbott had seen Liza's first show, *Best Foot Forward*, and when we suggested her for the part, he said, "I don't like the girl, but bring her in."

We taught her the song "A Quiet Thing" so it would be clear she was our choice. But when she came on during the audition, as she walked across the stage, Mr. Abbott said loudly, "Well, this is a waste of time!" His voice carried in the theater, and Liza heard him. There was a little hitch in her step, and she had that frightened-little-girl look that she gets. She sat down and sang, and after she finished, he said, "Thank you." But there was no way he was going to give her the part. And who was going to tell her? Mr. Abbott said, "You have to tell her, Fred. You made the biggest pitch for her." So I had to call and say, "Liza, you didn't get it." That was an awful phone call.

Liza Minnelli on auditioning for *Flora*:

George Abbott didn't want me, and Freddy was the one who had to call and tell me that I didn't have the part in *Flora*. Poor Freddy. I said, "Oh, that's okay," but I was dying inside.

EBB: But then a couple of weeks went by and—

KANDER: The actress who Abbott wanted was suddenly unavailable.

EBB: Eydie Gorme. He was going to have dinner with her

one night. At rehearsal the next morning—he was not an emotional guy—we asked him, "How did dinner go?" He said, "She never came," and that was it. He was really offended, and you knew she was out. Abbott went off to Florida, and we talked to Hal. Liza's name kept coming up, and Hal said, "Let me call Mr. Abbott."

KANDER: Mr. Abbott finally said, "Well, get me that Minnelli girl." Simple as that. His attitude was "We're professionals—"

EBB: "And we don't have to talk about it. Just get her." Now we were thrilled. I said, "Can I make that phone call?" So I called Liza and told her she had the part.

KANDER: Then Mr. Abbott fell completely in love with her.

EBB: Within a couple of weeks of rehearsals, he became her devoted slave.

KANDER: He really did. He would come back and sit in her dressing room night after night. He loved young talent. That really excited him. On Liza's birthday, Mr. Abbott came waltzing into a rehearsal with a cake, which was something he would never ordinarily do.

EBB: He loved the kind of singer she was. She could belt out that Karen Morrow thing.

KANDER: By the time we met him, he was slightly deaf. But he could certainly hear Liza.

EBB: I don't think she was ever less than aware of how important this show was for her, and Mr. Abbott was very protective of her. He insisted that Liza have an eleven o'clock number that we wrote out of town, "Sing Happy." She had to have a big song at the end.

KANDER: He was right. "Sing Happy" was the story of a woman who is literally having a nervous breakdown, whose world has collapsed around her, so that it was really screaming at somebody. The right way to do the song is in the context of the show. There was a concert in London once and a guy was singing it. He was singing it very well, but it didn't have a lot of meaning until I told him what the character in the show was feeling, and then he sang it and took your head off:

Sing me a happy song about robins in spring.
Sing me a happy song with a happy ending,
Some cheerful roundelay about catching the ring.
Sing happy.

Sing me a sonnet all about rolling in gold;
Some peppy melody about rainbows blending,
Nothing with phrases saying you're out in the cold.
Sing happy.

Tell me tomorrow's gonna be peaches and cream.
Assure me clouds are lined with a silver lining.
Say how you realize an impossible dream.
Sing me a happy song.

Play me a madrigal about trips to the moon,
Or some old ballad all about two eyes shining;
It can't be loud enough or a moment too soon,
Sing happy.

No need reminding me that it all fell apart,
I need no lyric singing of stormy weather;
There's quite enough around me that's breaking my heart,
Sing happy.

Give me a hallelujah and get up and shout,
Tell me the sun is shining around the corner;
Whoever's interested in helping me out,
Please keep it happy.

I'm only in the market for long, loud laughter,
I'll let you serenade me 'til dawn comes along;
Just make it a happy,
Keep it a happy song!

EBB: Another director might not have thought in terms of giving Liza a big number like that, but Mr. Abbott did because she was Liza and because of her notoriety. There was something notorious about her getting the role because she was Judy Garland's daughter.

KANDER: In writing for her, I don't think we ever thought in terms of her mother. We only thought of Judy as a kind of specter hanging over Liza. She was a controversial figure, and I guess in some ways still is. People would cruelly write that she was only getting work because she was her mother's daughter. That was always there, and I think Liza was terribly aware of it.

EBB: Judy came to the opening night of *Flora*. We had written the song "You Are You," and one of the lyrics was "You are not Myrna Loy, Myrna Loy is Myrna Loy. You are you." After the show, Judy came backstage and said to me, "Listen, I have a suggestion for that song. 'You are not *Judy Garland*, *Judy Garland* is *Judy Garland*. You are you.' That's what it should be." Then she turned around and walked away. I thought, my God, how amazing that she would say a thing like that. I later told Liza, and she was humiliated.

KANDER: She had the curse of being Judy Garland's daughter. She was always afraid that her mother would be in the audience and overshadow her. With the first nightclub act that she did, there was a question whether Judy was going to be there or not, and as I recall, Liza tried to get you to make sure she wasn't there. But her mother did show up, and that night Liza sat in front of her dressing mirror just shaking.

EBB: She was torn—"Do I introduce her? Do I not introduce her?" There were a couple of incidents. At the Waldorf-Astoria, Liza leaned down to her mother in the audience, and Judy literally grabbed her off the stage, then got up there with her. Liza sat on the side of the stage while Judy did two or three numbers, with the audience going crazy.

KANDER: When the two of them performed together and it was planned, that was different. But if it was a night that was supposed to be Liza's and her mother took over, that was difficult. The first time I saw that happen was the opening at the Waldorf, and Liza was sitting at her dressing table. Judy was there and she was drunk, sitting next to Liza. Judy said something like, "This is what we always wanted, isn't it, baby? This is our big night, baby. This is what we've always wanted." Liza just froze. I remember her face in the mirror, and it was one of those times I wished I was someplace else.

EBB: It was terrifying for her. She had anxiety attacks whenever she thought her mother was going to show up on any given night. That was sad. Ron Fields choreographed her act. We hired him because when he first approached us, he was wearing a sport coat with a red lining and Liza thought that was so spiffy. Marvin Hamlisch did all the arrangements. Marvin played for her and made all the musical selections. She sang "Pass that Peace Pipe." That was one of our big numbers. She also sang "Liza with a Z," and as I recall, she ended with "Sing Happy" from *Flora* as her finale.

KANDER: She also did "Maybe This Time."

EBB: What else did she sing? Oh, Sondheim's [*singing*] "It's a nice night and the mood's right / All I need now is the boy." At first her agents at MCA had hired another writer to do her act, a guy who had written for the McGuire Sisters. He was trying to write for Liza the way that he wrote for them. But he went away for a week, and in that time you and I wrote "Liza with a Z." I forget his name right now. I'm having a senior moment.

KANDER: Wilbur Evans.

EBB: That's right. No, it's not, but who cares? Wasn't Wilbur Evans in *Up in Central Park*?

KANDER: Well . . .

EBB: Well, maybe not. Who cares? After he left, I took over her act.

Liza Minnelli on "Liza with a Z":

Fred and John wrote that song in an hour or an hour and a half, and I learned it in an hour, which was impossible. "Liza with a Z" made the name Liza famous, and I'll always sing that song, just like I'll always sing "Maybe This Time."

KANDER: "Liza with a Z" was absolutely true. People were always calling her Lisa.

EBB: Writing the truth is what makes special material work.

KANDER: As a matter of fact, when she performed some years later at the Winter Garden, she wasn't sure whether it would be such a good idea to use that song again. But on the tickets for that show, her name was misspelled, which gave her the opportunity to say that night, "I thought I would never have to sing this song again, but if you look at your tickets . . ."

EBB: They had printed the tickets with only one "n" in Minnelli. I remember after *Flora* the first date that we played with Liza in concerts was the Shoreham Hotel in Washington. At that time, I didn't know anything about standing ovations. They were not something that happened every minute as far as I knew. At the end of our opening night, everyone in the audience stood up, and I thought, *Oh, my God, they're going home!* Liza thought they were going to the coat room. She stood there utterly bewildered and eventually sat down on the stage, overwhelmed by the response. She didn't know what to make of it, and I didn't either.

Ron Field was sitting with me, and he said, "They're standing up because they love her!"

KANDER: She was terrific in *Flora* because she was working with this absolute authority who was not going to put up with anything false. Mr. Abbott would not play that game. He really was crazy about her. He was the daddy that she needed.

EBB: But with Liza, when you let her loose, she's very creative. She has a deadly instinct for what will work with an audience. If you give her that freedom, you get the benefit of that expertise. On the other hand, if you are as dictatorial as Abbott, you don't get it. I think during *Flora* she wasn't ready to make that kind of contribution, even though she won a Tony Award for it. But later on, certainly during her TV special *Liza with a Z* and when she came into *Chicago*, she was ready. In 1993 I did her act *Stepping Out* at Radio City Music Hall, and we gave her the song "Seeing Things" from *The Happy Time*. She said, "I would like to close the first act with that song and show film clips of me and my father. I think that 'Seeing Things' is like our relationship. I was the practical one. He was the dreamer." She asked me, "Can I put that film together?"

Now, out of total trust for her instinct, I said, "Of course." She put the film together, and we could not have had a better closing for the first act. But Liza did that. Now, it could be that if George Abbott had been directing, he might not have let her. I didn't have a moment's doubt about Liza or about any of the other actors who were in *Flora*. Bob Dishy, Skipper Damon, and Mary Louise Wilson were perfect. I thought we were really lucky to have such a great cast.

KANDER: Mr. Abbott later said that he thought he was the person responsible for *Flora*'s not working.

EBB: I told Liza that I thought his love for her killed the show. He wouldn't allow that spunky side of her to come out.

KANDER: Mr. Abbott didn't want to see Liza do anything ugly or unseemly at all. The one thing that became very clear to us toward the end was that he couldn't bear the idea that Flora would be seriously in love with a Communist, because of his own political feelings.

EBB: He didn't relate to the material in that show because it was a world he never knew.

KANDER: He was rich when all these people were starving in the thirties.

EBB: He was playing golf with Whitney and his wealthy friends.

Harold Prince on *Flora*:

I always wanted to direct *Flora, the Red Menace*. I understood the milieu. I understood the characters. My wife's family had been victims of the blacklist, and I knew full well how idealistic and naive and innocent so many of the people who were pilloried really were, and I wanted the show to be about that and so did the original author of the novel. The problem was George Abbott didn't know anything about that. The guys started to write the score and Abbott heard it, and Abbott said, "It's brilliant. I want to direct that." And because of my relationship with him—I mean, without him I would not have gotten a strong foothold on a life in the theater—so, obviously, if he wanted to do it, it was his call. At that point in time, I didn't have the confidence, having not really done very much up until then, to know that I could have pulled it off. If I had had that confidence, I might have talked him out of it. Say I had done *Cabaret* first, and we were then working on this, I would have said, "Look, Mr. Abbott, you don't know these people." But I hadn't done that. And so of course he directed it, and I stayed on as the producer. But I always wish I had done it.

KANDER: Mr. Abbott was a terrific man, and I learned more about working in the theater from him than any other single source. At our first preview out of town, we were all standing in the back, and Mr. Abbott came in and looked at us rather strangely. We all recoiled at that moment, and he said, "All right, who's gonna sit with me? Can't learn about a show standing back there. Somebody's got to sit with me." I was closest and he grabbed my wrist. Then we sat down in the middle of the theater to experience what the audience reaction truly was. I've always remembered that. You can't stand removed from the audience and really know what they're feeling.

Mr. Abbott had a ritual whenever one of his shows opened. If the show was a hit, he would go to the party, drink a glass of wine, dance with his favorite chorus girl, and say, "Well, it worked out this time." If the show was a flop, he would have his glass of wine, dance with his favorite chorus girl, and say, "Well, this time it didn't work out." That was it. The ritual never changed. It's helped me a lot during flops to know they are part of what we do. Don't get too deceived by success, but don't get too deceived by a flop either.

EBB: We always deferred to Mr. Abbott. He removed the song "The Kid Herself" just because he thought it should go, and there was no forum or discussion about that. It was Liza's opening song, and he took it out and replaced it with another song that we had slated later, "All I Need Is One Good Break." It was not something I would have done because I was fond of "The Kid Herself" and I thought the number worked. I also wanted to start the show with Flora's high school graduation. But it was George Abbott, so naturally we did it his way.

KANDER: We had meetings every morning at the Ritz-Carlton Hotel in Boston—I remember you had to wear a tie to get into the hotel—and Hal would be there along with Mr. Abbott. You and I, who were staying someplace less impressive, put on ties and came to meetings every day. At one meeting, you had that idea for starting the show that you obviously believed in strongly, and I don't think any of us supported it. But you were very expressive, and finally Mr. Abbott said, "Well, let's try it. That's what we're here for." When the number was put in, the moment didn't really work, and Mr. Abbott said to you, "Look, we all decided to do this, so if it doesn't work, it's not your fault."

EBB: I was crestfallen.

KANDER: But he was considerate enough to protect your feelings. He said that to you before the show, didn't he?

EBB: I was grateful for that. It was kind of him not to say anything like, "Oh God, look at the time you've cost us."

KANDER: He asked us to write a new song for the same moment called "Among the People." We wrote it very fast in the theater while he was waiting for us downstairs. Then we played it, and he stopped the rehearsal and had us play it for the company. Afterwards, he said, "Isn't it amazing that these boys did this so fast!" He didn't have to offer that kind of praise, and I suspect another director like Jerry Robbins or Bob Fosse would not have done that.

EBB: I think he sensed our terror.

KANDER: Mr. Abbott was always a gentleman. I never saw him hurt anybody's feelings, except on purpose. If he couldn't get what he wanted after the third time, he would say something sharp, but it was never in a foot-stamping fury. Usually if he raised his voice, he would make it up with the person. He was the least self-indulgent director I've ever seen. I think that came out of his own sense of security, not that everything he did was going to be a hit.

EBB: It was terrifying to have our first Broadway show and so much riding on it—both our careers. I had already had an Off-Broadway show that didn't work. I worried that maybe nobody would want to hire me again, and you had done *A Family Affair*, which didn't work. But I doubt that you share this view.

KANDER: I don't think I thought in those terms. I just didn't want to do bad stuff. I had the same insecurities that everybody has, but I didn't think all that much about what would become of my life if we failed. Maybe I did and I've just forgotten.

EBB: The day after *Flora* failed, Mr. Abbott said something to us on the way out of the office. We literally had our hands on the doorknob, and he said, "Fellas." We both turned around, and he said, "You will work with me again, won't you?" Imagine what that meant coming from George Abbott.

KANDER: Our work routine was established then and hasn't changed to this day. I come to your house because you like staying home and I like going out, so it's an ideal arrangement. We usually work in the mornings. When I go home, I may think about the work, but it doesn't hang over me. You will worry over a piece and that may be because you stay in the same environment.

EBB: Over the years we've written in a number of ways. But usually we go into a room together with an idea and then start improvising.

KANDER: You have your large grand piano and a little piano. I've always much preferred working in a small room at the little piano.

EBB: It gives us propinquity. I'm usually at the desk next to the piano.

KANDER: We get up and walk around the room—

EBB: And we improvise.

KANDER: If we are working on a show, we talk about the moment that we're going to musicalize. Then maybe you will have a lyrical phrase and maybe I'll have a rhythmic idea. From then on, we improvise together. You never hand me a lyric and say, "Set this," and I never hand you a finished melodic chart and say, "Write a lyric to this." I would say that 90 percent of all the songs that we have written together we've written in the same room at the same time. Unlike most composers, we usually write the first song in a show first. It's not necessarily the most important song, but the opening of a show tells us something about what we're going to do with the score. It gives us a sense of the style in which we will be working. The idea very often comes from you, and it might be the first line or a title.

In those early days, working on *Flora* and *Cabaret*, we would basically improvise the scene before we would sit down to write, just to figure out the real emotions of the characters. Whenever we are writing for one or more characters in a show, we have to figure out what they are feeling, and we will sometimes even improvise in words to discover what they are really saying. I think we've always tried to be honest in our work, and if there is anything good about us, I hope it may be that we're not fake. To this day I don't think we write grandiose pieces to express something trite or frivolous, and we try not to be complicated just for the sake of being complicated. We have never really spoken about it, and I don't know if you will agree with this, but I like us most when we're most simple and direct.

EBB: I've never thought about it, but I suppose I feel that way too. It's the only way I know how to work. Just go right to it. I hope that our work is a little more than frivolous even when we set out to be frivolous. I like us when we can be funny and simple and touching.

KANDER: I suspect our favorite songs of those that we have written are probably quite different.

EBB: For performance, I think "And the World Goes 'Round" from the movie *New York, New York* is a very satisfactory song. In regard to special material, I think "Ring Them Bells" is very satisfactory.

KANDER: I agree with that one.

EBB: For a ballad, "Maybe This Time," which was used in the movie of *Cabaret* and then went into the show. You know I like belt songs, those where you just throw your head back and sing your ass off. You like more balladic pieces like "A Quiet Thing" in *Flora* and "My Own Space" from *The Act*. I like the ballads but they would never be my favorites.

KANDER: The big belt songs that we have written, some of which have done well and which you are fondest of, I sometimes refer to as screamers. Somebody's out there screaming, "Goddammit, world!"

EBB: Those get to me. I like to hear other people sing them, and when I was equipped to sing them, I liked singing them myself.

KANDER: Those songs are generally about *Life has kicked the shit out of me, but I'm going to live it*. We've written quite a few that express that theme and that may be what some people want to think of as a Kander and Ebb song, though there are certainly other songwriters who write them also.

Liza Minnelli on drawing inspiration from Kander and Ebb's songs:

There are times when I hang on to their songs emotionally. When I was coming off the medicine they put me on for my hip replacements, I was in such pain, but I knew I didn't want to take the medication. I knew that I would react differently to it than most people and become addicted. So I'm trying to get off this medicine and thinking, *Oh, for Christ's sake, it hurts, please take the pain away*. I kept going back to the lyrics of the first song of theirs I sang on the stage, "Unafraid," from *Flora, the Red Menace*: "Clouds may gather and swarm, yet this promise is made—we will weather this storm uniformly unafraid." Those words were inspiriting, and I use their songs in my life that way.

EBB: I do believe in that kind of message, not necessarily thematically in everything that we write, but it's there in my own mind. If I were writing a piece not connected to any particular show, I would generate that kind of thought. It's like Tony Newley's "Nothing Can Stop Me Now." That is the kind of song that most appeals to me. I don't even know if it's a good song, but I like what it says. Of course, I would be nowhere without your music to support that kind of lyric because all that energy you find when you sing a number like "And the World Goes 'Round" comes from the music. The words are one thing, but the music makes the words happen. I don't think you give yourself enough credit. You should but I can't talk you into it. I often wonder how you do what you do. I see you go to the piano and I listen to you play, but how do you go "dum dum da da dum" and make the song?

KANDER: Taking a spin off that as far as what makes the music happen, speaking strictly from a musical standpoint, I think harmony or harmonization is what helps melodic material to find itself. This is difficult to explain to someone who is not a musician, but if you just play a melody, unaccompanied and unharmonized, the ear will only hear some very bare-bones sounds. Maybe there will be implications of harmony, but once you harmonize it, the melody does something else. Jerome Kern's song "All the Things You Are" is a perfect example because the melody is really simple and wonderful while harmonically it is so adventurous. It takes you to so many interesting places that it's always commenting on itself. The song doesn't work without the harmony, or not nearly as well. Anybody whose fingers have twisted playing "All the Things You Are" will know what I mean.

On a different plane, it's the same way with Wagner. Often melodically what he's doing is very simple, while harmonically underneath it, he is telling us extraordinary things that we would not hear without it. When I work melodically, I'm also working harmonically at the same time. In other words, it's never a melody by itself that later I will harmonize. When something comes out melodically, all of the harmonic implications are there, at least in my head or my fingers. That's just my way of thinking about it.

EBB: All of that is totally mysterious to me. As you know, I don't read music or play the piano.

KANDER: It depends on what you hear in your head. I hear music all the time. I mean, *all the time*. Harmonization of a melody is a process that is happening continuously while I'm working, and if what I play at the piano sounds like bare bones to you, that is not what I'm hearing in my head.

EBB: I only hear rhythm.

KANDER: You're very good with rhythm. You often throw me into a rhythmic area that would not have occurred to me.

EBB: I love rhythm, whether it's in television commercials or in the theater or on a train, anytime and anywhere. Wherever there is rhythm, I'm happy.

THREE

Cabaret and *The Happy Time*

P roduced and directed by Harold Prince, *Cabaret* was based on John Van Druten's play *I Am a Camera* as well as Christopher Isherwood's stories about Weimar Berlin and the rise of Nazism. Prince commissioned Kander and Ebb for the score and Joe Masteroff for the book. The original cast featured Joel Grey (the epicene Emcee), Lotte Lenya (the gruff landlady), Jack Gilford (the Jewish grocer), Jill Haworth (the English cabaret singer Sally Bowles), and Bert Convy (the American writer). The show opened at the Broadhurst Theater on November 20, 1966, ran for 1,165 performances, and won eight Tonys, including Best Score for Kander and Ebb.

With its dark subject matter and innovative form—the phantasmagoric musical within a musical—*Cabaret* was hailed as a startling breakthrough that pushed musical theater into a more conceptualized realm. The songwriters added several new numbers— "Maybe This Time," "Mein Herr," and "Money, Money"—to Bob Fosse's 1972 film version, which refocused the drama for its stars, Liza Minnelli, Joel Grey, and Michael York. Under Harold Prince's direction, the first Broadway revival of *Cabaret* opened on October 29, 1987, and ran 262 performances despite being panned by *New York Times* critic Frank Rich.

A much revised version of the show returned to Broadway by way of London in 1998, choreographed by Rob Marshall and directed by both Marshall and Sam Mendes. New scenes were added, and four of the original Broadway songs were replaced by three from Fosse's movie and "I Don't Care Much," which had been cut from the original production. The musical became more daring and brazenly erotic. With the leads played by Natasha Richardson, Alan Cumming, Ron Rifkin, and Mary Louise Wilson, *Cabaret* was once again lauded as an exhilarating triumph.

●　○　●

KANDER: *Cabaret* evolved from Hal Prince's concept.

EBB: The concept was something that we were never as self-conscious about as the people who were guiding our careers were. We didn't have the idea of a concept musical in mind when we were writing *Cabaret*.

KANDER: We were just trying to write an entertaining piece.

EBB: It was made to order. Hal would say, "Maybe we should have a number here for this moment." We were working in a form which was very accessible to me, the revue form, where performers just come out and do a number. I was comfortable with that. I don't think that I appreciated the portentousness of the subject we were treating with a cabaret in Hitler's Berlin, or the seriousness of it, until that was pointed out to me.

KANDER: Unlike the integrated musical where everything grows in a very natural way out of each situation, Hal's musicals, beginning with *Cabaret*, are often a conceptual presentation with actors observing and songs that comment on the action. I think in a way that may have been his reaction to the more traditional musical form. His concept certainly influenced us a great deal.

EBB: It dictated our whole style. We were writing vaudeville.

KANDER: All of *Cabaret* is vaudeville.

EBB: Like a German music hall.

KANDER: What I remember most is that for months Hal and Joe Masteroff and you and I would sit in a room and play a game that I call "What if?" The director, writers, and composer sit in a room together and imagine the characters and elements of the story. That's an area where Hal's strength as a leader of collaboration shone through. We were inventing incidents that were going to be part of the story. What if such and such happens? What if somebody throws a brick through the window?

EBB: That was how we started to hammer out what the show would be. Out of those meetings came the Emcee, the master of ceremonies, as well as many of the theatrical devices that have worked to the show's enormous advantage.

KANDER: We wrote a long series of songs that we called "Berlin songs." We wrote many of those before the Emcee had been conceived, really. Initially they were going to be sung by different characters, and at some point in our conversations they were conceived for one person, the Emcee. That seemed like a really terrific solution. We wrote a lot of Berlin songs and we were fortunate that most of them were not used. "Wilkommen" was the first one.

EBB: That wasn't really a single song but a whole series of numbers. It was "Welcome to Berlin," and all these songs welcomed you to town. I don't remember specifically who thought of what because it was so collaborative in the backyard of Hal's house, sitting around with everybody just talking about what we hoped the show would be. At some point all these songs became one song sung by one person. I couldn't say specifically when that happened, but that was how it evolved and that was really the glory of that whole piece. I believe the idea of Sally's having an abortion came from you, but I couldn't swear to it. A brick being thrown through Herr Schultz's window—that may have come from me, though I'm not positive. But these were all events that came out in the shaping of the libretto. Joe's contribution was enormous. Of course, he wrote the damn thing while Hal and you and I threw pieces in. There was such joy in that process.

KANDER: It was to this day as far as I'm concerned the ideal way for collaborators to work on a piece.

EBB: I think *Cabaret* was the best collaborative process we ever had.

KANDER: Because eventually what that kind of work really means is that everybody ends up doing the same show. In other words, it's not the book writer doing one thing and you and I doing something else.

EBB: You know the horror of a musical is when you're out of town and the show's not working, and you get together and you find out, "Oh, my God, I didn't have that in mind!" Then you worry about how to fix it because you weren't writing the same piece.

KANDER: Hal was a master of that process. He was able to free us in a way that we all jumped in without any inhibitions whatsoever. If it was a bad idea, it was a bad idea. One of the reasons that we wrote so many songs for that piece is that we were writing our way into it. The more we wrote, the more we found out what the piece was. As the captain of the collaboration, Hal was able to be selective and to bring us together in agreement about what should be done.

EBB: Our songs were going to depend on those decisions. I think we knew that Hal had a kind of sublime faith in us, and that was terrifically inspiriting, to know that this master of the musical form believed that we could do it.

KANDER: I think in every show we've done, we've tried to at least partially re-create that with the "What if?" sessions.

EBB: It doesn't always work, but we hope for that. It depends most on having the right idea. *Cabaret* was the right idea. You work on other things with the same modus operandi, and if you have the wrong idea you don't succeed.

KANDER: Terrence McNally is a writer who also works that way with us. We often sit around this table with Terrence to plan out a piece. I don't know that we would know how to do a show if someone just handed us a script and said, "Put songs in it." We like having the director be captain.

EBB: Oh, it would be foolish to say, "Here's a script. Add songs." We should all agree this is how we do it.

Harold Prince on creating *Cabaret:*

We created a show with a character who I introduced to them, the Emcee, played by Joel Grey. He started out as this pathetic bad-taste entertainer and then became a Nazi. We had an early version that was a much more conventional musical in which basically that character came on and had a six-minute number during which he imitated all of the famous entertainers in Weimar Berlin. That summer I went off to Russia on vacation and saw a revue, *Ten Days That Shook the World*, and it shook me because it showed me that there was another way of structuring theater. It invited me to express myself as a director in ways I had not witnessed firsthand. I know there is nothing new under the sun, but this seemed new. When I came back, we took all those numbers and peppered them throughout the show, dividing the stage between the real world and a limbo world. I suppose it was a brave design, but it was personal and thus exciting to contemplate. *Cabaret* influenced the form of many Broadway shows, including other Kander and Ebb shows, not just *Zorba* and *Chicago* but *The Act* as well. Now, oddly enough, that concept has almost become a cliché. But that's what happens.

KANDER: Researching *Cabaret*, I listened to German jazz and vaudeville songs more than anything else, and then I just forgot about it. On any show, I may listen to the music of a particular style or a region, and then I forget all about it. I trust that there will be some kind of stylistic influence in what I'm doing, but it's a thing I do unconsciously while listening.

EBB: For that show I read as much as I could and listened to as much as was available to me, much of which you supplied. We would listen to those German vaudeville numbers, and songs like "Two Ladies" stemmed directly from that process. We filter all of that through our own sensibility and out comes what we do. Sometimes people don't realize that. With the song "Tomorrow Belongs to Me," I received letters accusing me of using an actual Nazi anthem. That was completely false.

KANDER: There were people who claimed they had heard the song in Nazi Germany—

EBB: They said, "How dare you put that on the stage!" But the song didn't exist before we wrote it. Of course, there is always an unconscious element as well. I dream all the time. While we were working on *Cabaret*, I had a dream one night that took place on the set of *Hello, Dolly*. Joel Grey came out with a gorilla in a tutu, and it kept walking around the apron. I thought, *My God, how wonderful that is!* It's baroque. It's bizarre. It was everything that I could have wanted. So I told you about it, and you also loved the image. But then you asked me a key question, "Well, what's the song?"

KANDER: Right. What's the song about?

EBB: That never occurred to me. I called Hal Prince on the phone, and I said, "Hal, I want to do a number for Joel and a gorilla!" He said, "Oh, that's great. What's it about?" Again, I didn't know. Hal was like a god and mentor to me. If he had said, "I don't think that will work," for whatever reason he might have had, I would have killed it. But he giggled and said, "That sounds like fun. What's it about?" I realized that the two people who meant the most to me, you and Hal, both asked the same pertinent question. Then I really had to think of what the number was about. I wanted it to be about anti-Semitism, and it all worked from there, to show how anti-Semitism had crept into the cabaret. That was my intent, and eventually the line "If you could see her through my eyes, / She wouldn't look Jewish at all" generated the whole number:

I know what you're thinking,
You wonder why I chose her
Out of all the ladies in the world.
That's just a first impression,
What good's a first impression?
If you knew her like I do,
It would change your point of view.

If you could see her through my eyes,
You wouldn't wonder at all.
If you could see her through my eyes,
I guarantee you would fall (like I did).
When we're in public together,
I hear society moan,
But if they could see her through my eyes,
Maybe they'd leave us alone.

How can I speak of her virtues?
I don't know where to begin.
She's clever, she's sweet, she reads music,
She doesn't smoke or drink gin (like I do).
Yet when we're walking together,
They sneer if I'm holding her hand,
If they could see her through my eyes,
Maybe they'd all understand.

I understand your objection,
I grant you my problem's not small;
But if you could see her through my eyes,
She wouldn't look Jewish at all.

KANDER: One of the things about Hal generally in our work with him, as opposed to a lot of other smart directors, you could never be too bold for him. You could never have an idea too brazen or too far out. He was never going to say, "Oh no, we mustn't do that."

EBB: He was not cowed by anything.

KANDER: The bolder the better.

EBB: Except once in *Cabaret*. During tryouts, that line, "She wouldn't look Jewish at all," got the exact reaction that I had hoped for from the audience. There was a collective gasp, which was followed by a moment of silence, and then applause. But when we were about to open in New York, we received a letter from a rabbi who claimed to represent millions of Jews. He found the line decidedly anti-Semitic and threatened to encourage all the Jewish groups to boycott us if it wasn't changed. This same rabbi had earlier disrupted a performance in Boston apparently because he was outraged that a swastika appeared in the show.

At the first preview, I walked into the lobby of the theater, and a lady wearing a checkered skirt accosted me: "Do you have anything to do with this show?" I told her that I wrote the lyrics, and she said, "Well, I represent the B'nai B'rith, and we are here to protest the use of that line 'She wouldn't look Jewish at all.' You are suggesting that Jewish women look like gorillas. That is blatantly anti-Semitic, and if you don't take it out, we will cancel all of our theater parties." The truth is, after that we ran scared. I was frightened. Hal was frightened, and he is not someone who is easily intimidated.

KANDER: But that wasn't Hal the director. That was Hal the producer.

EBB: It might have killed his career. He needed that hit as much as we did. *Cabaret* was one of his early chances to be a successful director. He was also the producer, and a producer depends on theater parties, especially at the beginning of the run. We were all so desperate to succeed that we did things that we would never do today. Coming up with another punch line was one of the most difficult tasks that I have ever faced in the theater. I rewrote it as "She isn't a *meeskite* at all."

KANDER: *Meeskite*—an ugly person—didn't have the same meaning at all. *Meeskite*—like, so what?

EBB: Whenever Joel Grey thought that he could get away with it, especially if he knew that someone important to us was in the audience, he would sing, "She wouldn't look Jewish at all." Afterwards, the stage manager would yell at him, and then he would say, "It just slipped out!"

KANDER: Decisions which are made under pressure like that—*meeskite* was one—are almost always regretted. They rarely ever serve the purpose that people intended. Can you think of a moment where we have made a change after the fact where a song was actually improved?

EBB: No. But I remember changing a lyric so we got a bigger laugh.

KANDER: That's different. I mean changing something because people insist that you can't do that.

Harold Prince on cutting Ebb's controversial lyric:

During the first previews, the show would end and people would stay in the audience arguing with one another. The subject was almost invariably Fred's lyric "She wouldn't look Jewish at all." The decision of whether to change the line was mine. I was where the buck stopped, and I said, "I am not going to jeopardize this show over this line. And you know what? If it's cowardly of me, it's cowardly of me, but the show is too important." It was a pragmatic decision on my part, and I've never regretted that I did it. I think Freddy has always regretted that I did it, and perhaps John also. But on the other hand, a few years later when they made the film, the line was restored. The show had been a huge success and I've always felt that just the few years separating it from the film made things more acceptable than they would have been originally.

EBB: We changed the intent of the song with the word *meeskite*. But Bob Fosse put the original line back in for the movie. The screen went quiet, and Joel said it. The scene was shot that way because if there had been any protest, Joel could have dubbed in another line. But in the movie, the line was accepted. That reminds me that in the original *Cabaret*, when we knew Jack Gilford, playing the Jewish grocer, was scheduled to have a moment at his engagement party, and I came up with *meeskite* and wrote the song, Jack was right there in the room with us. Working that closely with a performer, we can hear the way he speaks and sings, and we can see his facial expressions. We knew what he would do with the song physically, like lifting back the covers to look at the newborn baby and saying she was gorgeous. We knew how funny he could make that moment. It's telling that the number had to be religiously cut after Jack stopped performing it.

KANDER: He made a terrific moment of it, but it was so Gilfordesque that we finally took it out of the revival. Nobody else could make it happen.

EBB: Nobody else made it funny. You would think that Jack made the blueprint for that moment and that other people could play it because it was foolproof, but it was never the same without him. I also miss Lotte Lenya in that show. That was such a wonderful relationship we had with her, and she was the perfect embodiment of that role. There have been other people who have played that role who were wonderful, but we wrote it for her.

KANDER: She was the conscience of *Cabaret*, really.

EBB: It was Hal's idea to cast her.

KANDER: That was an idea we all leapt at.

EBB: We wrote it with Lenya's voice in mind, knowing that when she walked on the stage, she brought with her the validation of the period and the sound. She personified the authenticity of what we were doing.

KANDER: She said something to me once that I've always cherished. We were out of town with *Cabaret* and I knew what had already started to happen, that I would be accused of ripping off Kurt Weill. But the fact is that in the preparation for that show, I deliberately stayed away from listening to Kurt Weill. I said to Lenya before we opened, "When the reviews come out, I know that they're going to say that I was cribbing from Kurt Weill, but I just want you to know that was never my intention." She was a great sympathizer. I remember she took my head in her hands and said, "No, no, it's not Kurt. When I'm on the stage, it's Berlin that I hear when I sing your songs." I thought, if she feels that way, then fuck everybody else. It meant a very great deal to me.

EBB: She told me, "You remind me of Kurt. You sweat." She loved that I sweated.

KANDER: Lenya was such a strong person, and yet at the same time, I always felt that she was physically very fragile. She looked like those bones might break at any minute. Lenya was also very supportive of Jill Haworth when Jill got bad reviews and the show didn't. Lenya took her under her wing and showed her all of her own old bad reviews. She was always a big fan of Jill's.

EBB: I never understood the criticism that Jill received. Walter Kerr was brutal to her, and I never thought that was justified at all. We saw a lot of people for that role, but Hal was determined that Sally Bowles be English.

KANDER: Hal flew me to London to hear Sarah Miles early on when she was being considered for the role. That was a weird experience. She was living with a writer, Robert Bolt, and after I arrived, they were terribly nice to me and took me out to dinner. I told her, "I really just need to hear you sing, if we can sit down somewhere." They couldn't have been sweeter, but they always had other things to do. Robert Bolt said, "Oh, Sarah sings just fine," and she said that about herself too. We finally went to a little church. She didn't have anybody to play for her, but she said, "I'll sing for you in here." She stood at the front of the church and started to sing. I was at the back of the church and couldn't hear her. I kept moving closer and closer without realizing it until I was practically in her face and still couldn't hear her. I had to report back to Hal that she was *not* a singer. But he was willing to sacrifice a lot in order to have an English girl play that part.

EBB: With that show we had a lot to prove coming off a bomb like *Flora*.

KANDER: We wrote many Berlin songs before Joel Grey came into it, but we wrote more after he was involved. It helped me enormously to have people like Lotte Lenya and Jack Gilford in the back of my mind. As you know, Jack was a great buddy of Zero Mostel's. I had done stock with Zero back in the fifties when there were many places he couldn't work because of the blacklist. I was conducting, and I'll never forget this. He was in *Kismet* playing a scene with Bill Johnson, and Zero had a piece of business that was hilarious. It got a huge laugh that lasted fifteen seconds. By the end of the week, it lasted ten minutes, and he went on and on ad-libbing to the point that Bill Johnson knocked him to the floor of the stage. I mean, Bill really hit him. Zero went down with a thud, then got right up, and the scene went on as if nothing had happened. There are two comic geniuses I've worked with in my life. Zero was one, and Beatrice Lillie was the other. It was awful for the writer, but they could take any piece of business and invent and invent.

EBB: I imagine some writers consider themselves lucky to get those laughs that they haven't really earned themselves, that are delivered for them by another personality.

KANDER: Zero was very hard on Jack Gilford, wasn't he?

EBB: In *A Funny Thing Happened on the Way to the Forum*. But Jack never complained about anything. He once told me,

"There's no controlling Zero. He actually took me by the shoulders at one point and turned my back to the audience so he could do a piece of business. I couldn't even see what Zero was doing. I only knew I was facing scenery when I should have been facing an audience." He did that time after time. The trouble with Zero was that very few people stood up to him.

KANDER: He was an awesome physical presence.

EBB: People were afraid of him.

KANDER: You know how he was controllable? He was very controllable musically. He had a great respect for music, and in my dealings with him if I said anything to correct him, he would do it instantly. Working in stock, there was a director who was nasty to one of the kids in the chorus. One time when he was being especially unpleasant, Zero stopped the rehearsal and picked him up by his necktie. Zero said, "I don't ever want to hear you talking to a member of this company like that again." That was all there was to it. Zero did have a sense of justice.

EBB: When he lived in my building, the San Remo, we had an elevator strike once, and the tenants had to sign up for doorman duty. I signed up to be a doorman, and Zero signed underneath me and put an arrow next to my name with the line, "When he works, I'll work." We were on one night together, and he was just darling. Humble and sweet. A great conversationalist. When he came to see *Chicago* in premiere, I remember how gracious he was about praising us for our work. He was almost teary about it. That was a Zero very few people got to see because when he was up on the stage he was just a buffoon, but when he was off he was a gentle, funny man.

KANDER: Zero said something memorable when we were doing stock together. Before the last show, he threw his great, beefy arm around my shoulder and said, "Kander, I want you to do me a favor. Every morning when you get up, I want you to look in the mirror and say, 'My name is John Kander and I'm a talented man, and fuck 'em all.' " I was pretty timid in those days and I can't tell you what that meant to me. I told him later outside the theater when *Chicago* opened how I always remembered that advice. Then he went around telling everyone, "I'm responsible for his entire career!" But I feel the same as you do. I loved him, that wonderful, impossible bear of a man.

EBB: We were extremely fortunate with the revivals of both *Chicago* and *Cabaret*, the most recent ones, but the fact is if I go see *Cabaret* today, I know I would want to change things. I saw *Chicago* recently and there were moments where I thought I could have written a better line, where I didn't think a number was as good as it ought to be. Among other things that you taught me is to leave well enough alone. Don't mess with it. I have to let it be because I may in fact ruin a number by refusing to leave it alone.

KANDER: Whenever you have a revival, you always find things that you want to change. When *Cabaret*, the show, first came out, it was considered highly innovative and it later influenced other shows. But by the time the first revival was mounted in 1987, it no longer seemed new to people. Even with some changes in the score and staging, it was more or less a re-creation of the original production.

EBB: Many people had already been exposed to it with the movie.

KANDER: In a way, Sam Mendes's current production is like a renewed experience. The show suddenly seems innovative and daring in the way the original production seemed. But this same production in ten years would probably look very tired if we remounted it.

EBB: It would probably look tame in ten years.

KANDER: Sam's production was done in London in 1993 at the Donmar Warehouse before it came to New York—

EBB: But I don't think seeing it at the Donmar you would

for a second have thought the show would become the kind of hit that it has become. Sam's artistry was not all that apparent to me then. I could see the production was very well done, but I thought the leading lady was terribly miscast, and I didn't like it a hell of a lot.

KANDER: Oh, I did, though she was all wrong. I thought Sam's concept was just brilliant, but it was made immensely better by Rob Marshall when it came to New York, and it was essentially the same concept. In the original *Cabaret*, we actually had two different orchestras. Within one large orchestra, there was the cabaret orchestra, and whenever we were doing a number there was a certain number of instruments that we used for that particular piece, and whenever we were doing integrated songs for scenes outside the Kit Kat Club, the orchestra was a different orchestra. That was all deliberate.

Orchestrally, I think this current production of *Cabaret* is ingenious because the orchestrator, Michael Gibson, created an orchestration which has more instrumental parts than we have performers. The entire cast is now the orchestra. All the performers have to play an instrument, and if one of the actors who is performing that evening plays the harp, she has a harp part, and if not, she will play another instrument. I don't know how Michael did it even though we talked about it endlessly. You can recast that show all over the place and still have an orchestra and be able to switch instruments.

One of the reasons I don't orchestrate is that I'm not very good at it. I can orchestrate if I have to, but not wonderfully. It's also very time-consuming. You can't stay home and orchestrate and go to rehearsal and write. All that you can do is supervise. Michael is like a musical right arm. What I get from him is exactly what I intend musically instead of someone coming in and trying to improve me. We will often talk on the phone, and he may say something like, "I hear an oboe here." Then both of us will imagine hearing that, and I may say, "That sounds good, but what if we tried . . ." We go back and forth that way. Since *Woman of the Year*, Michael has done most of our shows and we have a wonderful relationship. I assume Steve Sondheim has a similar kind of relationship with Jonathan Tunick.

EBB: In the new production, the audience was seated at tables and chairs in the Kit Kat Club instead of in the theater. But seeing it in London, we had never dreamed, *Oh, my God, wait until New York sees this!* When finally I did see the show in New York, I had just gotten out of the hospital and I went with Chita. You were there that night sitting next to us. It may have been the first preview.

KANDER: I went back many times.

EBB: I walked in and those girls were walking around dressed the way they do, and kind of sniffing at the audience. And I wept. I looked at that show and what I saw overwhelmed me, what Sam had done. I had no idea it would be like that. Who would have imagined pineapples coming down from the ceiling in "The Pineapple Song." There were so many arresting moments like that. Chita grabbed my hand, which made it worse, may I tell you. You know I cry a lot.

KANDER: We cry at different things.

●   ○   ●

Two years after their success with *Cabaret*, Kander and Ebb had a less than happy experience with David Merrick's production of *The Happy Time*, with a book from N. Richard Nash. Under the direction of Gower Champion, the musical was turned into a multimedia extravaganza that overshadowed its stars, Robert Goulet and David Wayne. *The Happy Time* opened at the Broadway Theater, January 18, 1968, and ran for 286 performances. Despite the charms of the score and two Tony Awards for Champion and one for Goulet, the show became one of Broadway's first million-dollar flops.

• ◦ •

KANDER: Collaboration is the most difficult part of our business, where collaboration involves the director, producer, writers— everyone who is in a key position creatively on a show. During our collaboration on *The Happy Time*, the concept of the show changed in a way that disappointed us when we were in Los Angeles. That was the wrong place for us to be trying out that show because people were saying, "You can't have Robert Goulet play a failure"—meaning, his character in the script. Our director, Gower Champion, lost confidence in what the story was about, and Dick Nash had written a beautiful script. But we changed the show out of town in certain ways that we didn't like.

EBB: I remember that Gower accepted some hideous advice from his Los Angeles friends. *The Happy Time* was a tough little libretto, and rightly so, reminiscent of *The Rainmaker* in that the story essentially involved exposing fraud, but with much warmth and humor. Bob Goulet played a French Canadian man, Uncle Jacques, who for years has deceived his family into thinking he is something he is not. At the end, he has to confess to his fourteen-year-old nephew, Bibi, who idolizes him, that he wasn't really a glamorous photographer, that he was just a failure.

KANDER: He was actually a photographer who took pictures of shoes. The experience was sad because of what the show became, especially for Dick Nash, who was the real victim in the way they changed his book and the whole character for Goulet as the uncle.

EBB: With the original story in mind, we wrote the song "Please Stay" to show the relationship between Uncle Jacques and his nephew. Uncle Jacques returns to French Canada to visit

his family, and it is the opinion of the family that he is a bad influence on the boy. But Bibi adores him and one night Uncle
Jacques takes him out on the town. They have a really wonderful
time, and then they come home. They are in the room they share,
and the song is sung by the boy to reveal what he feels about
his uncle, who is planning to leave. Bibi protests, not wanting his
uncle to return to his glamorous life:

I read a book on London.
It's beautiful, I know.
Such fun to be in London:
Don't go.

And Lisbon must be pretty
Around this time of year.
Just marvelous in Lisbon:
Stay here.

And Venice takes your breath away,
They say.
Stay!

It's dumb for you to stick around
When you could be in Rome.
Please stay home.
Vienna, so you tell me, is just your kind of town.
Romantic old Vienna:
Sit down.

And Paris has the fountains,
The churches and the Louvre,
So everyone loves Paris:
Don't move.

In Hong Kong oriental splendors wait,
Wait!

Each night in New York City
Is a lot like New Year's Eve.
But please don't leave.
I know you'll never do it
but I'm asking anyway,
Please, please stay!

KANDER: Not only were the book and the character changed, but Gower had devised a production scheme involving rear projections, which sounded very beautiful but turned out to be unbelievably destructive. At that time the only way you could have rear projections appear big on screen was to play in the biggest theater in New York.

EBB: Anyone standing in front of the projector cast a huge shadow.

KANDER: The projections were gorgeous. Unfortunately, they dwarfed the actors and the show was just swallowed.

EBB: Like *The Glass Menagerie* at Radio City Music Hall.

KANDER: *The Happy Time* should have been done in a more intimate space. I think we were all party to what happened because when Gower first described what he wanted to do, it sounded magical and we went along with the idea.

EBB: It was a new projection technique that he had seen at the Montreal World's Fair.

KANDER: A few years later we had the chance to rewrite some of the score, and Dick Nash had the chance to have his book put back. When that show was revived at the Goodspeed Opera House, it became a piece that I quite liked.

EBB: I thought it was much improved.

KANDER: I don't know if you agree with this, but when we

previewed the original production in Los Angeles, we played a long time and it was quite successful. But Los Angeles audiences do not really help a show going to Broadway. I don't think you can learn from a Los Angeles audience what you need to learn for a New York production.

EBB: I agree. David Merrick came to see the show once in Los Angeles. He trusted his creative team and he made a point about that, telling us, "If I trust you, I don't have to come to see the show." But when he finally did see the show, he was very unhappy, and we had difficulties. But he made most of the difficulties for Gower, not for us. At one point Gower said, "When we get to Los Angeles, David will see the show and then threaten to close us at the Ahmanson unless we make changes. Don't worry about him. Just stay out of it, Fred. I'll take care of David." After a few weeks in Los Angeles, David Merrick called me and said, "I'm ready to close the show. Gower won't make the changes I want, and I'm closing this show unless you can influence him." I said, "Oh, Mr. Merrick, I wouldn't know how to do that." Of course, Merrick didn't close the show, but Gower had predicted it almost to the day.

KANDER: Gower in that situation was quite the opposite of the way he was later when we worked with him on *The Act*. During *The Happy Time*, we had to stay away from rehearsals until he had finished a piece and was ready to present it.

EBB: We were staying way on the other side of Los Angeles, and we were forbidden to come except for one day when he finally said he had a number that we could see. We went down to the space where he was rehearsing, and at the entrance there were huge black curtains.

KANDER: In order to enter this place, instead of going in through a door, we had to go through curtains.

EBB: It was like going into some triple-X porno house. We had to pull aside these layers of thick black curtains, and then we kept going in and eventually arrived in the rehearsal space. Gower and his assistant had them perform a song for us called "Without Me," and we thought it was just wonderful.

KANDER: One of the best numbers I've ever seen in my life.

EBB: We were thrilled, and then we were dismissed. We went home and didn't see Gower again during rehearsals. He never let us come again. Jerry Herman had warned me to expect that. Gower never let him into *Hello, Dolly*. Jerry said, "Fred, all I can tell you is it will be worth it."

KANDER: There was a moment that I will always remember fondly. I was living in the house that you had rented and have since bought in California. It belonged to Rhonda Fleming and had been furnished by her. In the living room there were several ornate lamps with enormous cylindrical shades that hung down very low. Gower came by one day to go over the script, and it was just the three of us. It was daylight when he arrived, near the end of the afternoon. As we were sitting together, reading and talking, it kept getting darker and darker. So we turned on the lights.

EBB: Night had fallen.

KANDER: Without any of us saying anything about it, we slowly ended up on the floor with the scripts under the lampshade, huddled around that little pool of light. At which point Gower looked up and said with his dry, deadpan manner, "Rhonda doesn't read much, does she?"

EBB: There really was no light in the house. For me *The Happy Time* was one of the saddest experiences of our collaboration because I loved that show—Dick's book as well as what we had written. I adored Bobby Goulet, and I thought the show would be fine. But the opening night in New York was a disaster. Clive Barnes was then the leading theater critic for the *Times* and a really essential review, and he was late arriving. So the curtain was being held for him.

KANDER: He was a lot late.

EBB: It got to be like a half hour, then forty minutes, then forty-five minutes, and David Merrick went down the aisle to speak to one of the other critics. I heard that critic say, "David, would you have held the curtain for me if I was late?" We could feel the hostility among the critical fraternity, all of whom were gathered to review the piece. Clive eventually showed up almost an hour late. If the poor guy had written a rave, they would have said he was atoning for his unpardonable sin.

KANDER: But he wrote a favorable review.

EBB: It was a clever, pleasant review. I don't think it sold any tickets. He straddled the fence, but he was in a tough spot.

KANDER: After *Happy Time* opened, I went on a holiday, and on my return the plane was delayed in Antigua. There was a *Time* magazine at the airport newsstand, and I thought, *Oh, that critic always hates our work.* But I kept circling the newsstand and finally said to myself, "I'll just open it and turn to the table of contents, and if there is a theater section, I won't buy it." So I opened the magazine to the table of contents and for that week only, as if for my benefit, *Time* was trying a new format putting capsule reviews on the contents page. At the top, there was a sentence that jumped out at me: "Songs so undistinguished they scarcely deserve to be sung out loud." I had to laugh because I had spent all that time torturing myself about whether to look at the magazine. I've never forgotten that.

EBB: I think when it comes to critics that you tend to love them when they like you and hate them when they don't.

KANDER: Some are better than others, but I can't recall any critic writing a piece that was such a revelation that it illuminated a show for me. Of course, when you're out of town and you get reviews that all point to a particular moment in the first act, then you have to figure that moment out. I usually feel better about critics after we finally come into New York. But you and I are different about this. I really don't have to read reviews. I'll want to know whether they were good or bad, but I don't feel compelled to read a bad review. Of course, I need to know if the *Times* pans a show of ours, but I won't search through the trash to make sure that I've read it. Sometimes they say hurtful things that you remember for the rest of your life.

EBB: With a critic who has been consistently mean about your work, sometimes all you can do is hope to outlive him. We had fun at the expense of critics with a number that we wrote for *Curtains*, which we're finally doing as a workshop for the Nederlanders.

KANDER: *Curtains* is really old. We started that piece about fourteen years ago.

EBB: Peter Stone originally had a title, *Who Killed David Merrick?*

KANDER: We started writing that piece when David Merrick was still alive. That's how long we've been working on it. Actually, the fact is nobody wanted to do it until now.

EBB: We never really showed it to anybody. It's always been one of your trunk musicals. Peter wanted to write a murder mystery that took place in a musical on the way to New York. The show inside the show is a musical comedy out of town. When the company opens in Boston, the producer is murdered. It's a farcical whodunit.

KANDER: Everybody has a reason to kill him. *Curtains* is strange because one of the leading characters is a detective who is in love with show business. In his monologues, he is often quoting lines from famous musicals like *Carousel*.

EBB: He's an amateur musical performer in addition to being a detective.

KANDER: He's played leading roles at his little local community theater, and now he's thrilled to have landed in the middle of Boston's Colonial Theater to investigate the murder. It's a terminally silly piece.

EBB: We wrote a song called "What Kind of Man" for a

scene after the musical comedy opens in Boston and members of the company listen to the reviews. After hearing how one critic has panned the show, the company members sing about critics:

What kind of man would take a job like that?
    What kind of slob would take a job like that?
Who could be mean enough?
    Base and obscene enough?
To take a job like that?

What kind of man would take a job like that?
    What kind of clown would put you down like that?
Who could be vile enough?
    Bulging with bile enough?
To take a job like that?
Oh, what kind of low-down dirty bum?
    Oh, what kind of swinish, scurvy scum
Loathsome as they come.
    I wonder . . .

What kind of man would take a job like that?
What kind of snake would drive the stake like that?
Who could be jerk enough?
Hard up for work enough?
To want a job like that?

What kind of man would want a job like that?
What kind of putz would squeeze your nuts like that?
Who could be low enough?
Needing the dough enough?
To want a job like that?

E B B : The tone suddenly changes after a member of the company reads a good review from the *Harvard Crimson*:

What kind of genius has a mind like that?
So perspicacious, wise and kind like that?
Far from his mother's knee
She must be thrilled to see
How he grew up to be
Such lovely company.
Others are stinkers,
There are a few heavy thinkers,
So it lifts up your heart
To meet a man like that.

KANDER: That last part was an afterthought because we didn't know how to end the piece. Our hearts were in the first part. As I've said, we really always have a good time when we're writing, but this kind of song, which is full-out nasty and vitriolic, is a very special kind of good time.

EBB: Those are funny rhymes. It's a show that is mostly about words and jokes.

KANDER: I think the book and lyrics are funny, but musically I have a lot of work to do. The question with *Curtains* is whether the humor is so theatrically focused, so show business oriented, that it may not be funny to other people. I'm curious about that. I don't know whether it's going to be a show that will work practically in a commercial theater.

EBB: You never know. I hope something happens with it, but if not, at least we've had a good time working on it. We're writing about what's classically wrong with the theater, and your opinions about critics and show business personalities are sort of eternal.

FOUR

Zorba and *70, Girls, 70*

K ander and Ebb teamed up with Harold Prince again on *Zorba*, working from a script by Joe Stein that was based on the Nikos Kazantzakis novel. Utilizing a conceptual approach similar to that used in *Cabaret*, Prince unfolded the story as a tale told by café entertainers. Kander and Ebb's score effectively adapted Greek folk music to the expectations of their Broadway audience. Writing deftly for character and situation, the songwriters were attracted to the show's dark Cretan atmosphere. They instilled their score with fire ("Life Is"), humor ("No Boom Boom"), and tenderness ("Happy Birthday to Me").

With a cast that featured Herschel Bernardi and Maria Karnilova, the show opened at the Imperial Theater on November 17, 1968, and played for 305 performances. *Zorba* was ultimately too dark for most Broadway audiences. A revival in 1983 attempted to be more upbeat and was more successful commercially, thanks primarily to its star, Anthony Quinn. Quinn was joined by Lila Kedrova, who won a Tony when she stepped into the Karnilova role as the fading French courtesan, Madame Hortense. The revival was directed by Michael Cacoyannis, who had also directed the 1964 movie *Zorba the Greek*, in which Quinn and Kedrova played the leads.

● ● ●

KANDER: *Zorba* began while we were working on *The Happy Time*—

EBB: And sharing a house in California. The infamous Rhonda Fleming place.

KANDER: Hal Prince asked us to read *Zorba the Greek*.

EBB: That tome.

KANDER: We read the book and then Hal called to find out what we felt about it, and what we felt initially was not good.

EBB: And it was very long, a long tome.

KANDER: Hal said, "Wait a minute, let me describe the opening scene for you."

EBB: You know how that little old lady on *Golden Girls* says, "Picture this!" Then she tells the story. Hal was like that, very excited. "Picture this! This is how the opening is going to be."

KANDER: By the time he finished describing the opening, he had us.

EBB: We thought it was fabulous, and he called it a "bouzouki parlor." But there is no such thing.

KANDER: Yes, a bouzouki circle, which doesn't exist.

EBB: He made it up and we bought it because we didn't know any better.

KANDER: The opening had a wonderful look. The stage was filled with smoke, and you heard the sound of instruments behind the curtain.

EBB: And the whole cast was lined up—

KANDER: In a circle with the dark lady in the middle. The entire cast was sitting there, saying, "What do we do now?" They finally decided to tell the story of Zorba. A few of these characters telling the story were always onstage watching.

EBB: Hal loves observing on the stage, where people are placed around and just watching the action. In *Zorba*, he used that device throughout.

KANDER: I thought Hal's staging was superb. We never

fully appreciated how wonderfully he directed that show until we saw what Michael Cacoyannis did to it when he staged the revival. I sent a note to Hal when we went into rehearsals for the revival, saying, "I finally realize the flypaper that you were walking on." Cacoyannis had also directed the film. In Hal's original show, we were very careful about keeping away from the movie. There were lines that had to be taken out of Joe Stein's script because they were in the screenplay.

EBB: We were under some legal stricture.

KANDER: As I recall, it had to do with the fact that Mrs. Kazantzakis and Cacoyannis were not on good terms. But she was a supporter of the stage piece. It was the novel that guided us, and Kazantzakis's letters, which contained wonderful material from the real Zorba.

EBB: There were moments in that show, I think, that are among the best-realized musical moments in our careers, such as when Maria Karnilova as Madame Hortense is dying, and Hal gave her a moment where she's on her deathbed. But she gets up and she's like a girl again, singing the song "Happy Birthday to Me."

KANDER: And at the end of the song, she goes back to the bed—

EBB: And dies. That was absolutely killing for me, breathtaking. I think we managed to come up with a decent musicalization there, but even without that, it was a stunning idea.

KANDER: Karnilova was marvelous doing it.

EBB: In the revival, Lila Kedrova played Madame Hortense. She was lovely, but I found her a little taxing because her English was very limited. I think on the screen she could get away with it because you were practically in her mouth, and if nothing else you could lip-read her part.

KANDER: She was very good in "Happy Birthday."

EBB: That's just a good moment, and you've really got to

act well, and she could do that. She could act everything we gave her.

KANDER: But Karnilova for me was way superior. She had a moment in the original production after she sings the song "Only Love," and she had a cross with an umbrella, and the music goes on a long time. She just crossed to stage right and you couldn't take your eyes off her. She had that compelling quality which only a great dancer can have. That I will always remember.

EBB: "The Crow" was another rich moment, where all the old ladies realize that she's sick. It was a ritual in Crete that the neighbors pick the house clean when they know somebody is dying, and Hal staged that beautifully. There were moments like that, and yet overall, I didn't take as much pleasure in the show as I did in some of the other pieces we've written.

KANDER: Well, you turned on it when it didn't do well.

EBB: Maybe I did. I've admitted how success-oriented I am.

KANDER: But I think you're right about one thing. The best-realized element in the show was the conception of Madame Hortense. The whole business when she's singing to Zorba and Nikos about the past with the song "No Boom Boom," and Hal had the four admirals standing behind the Victrola singing. Hal had a real take on that piece, though I think the original set was heavy.

EBB: The whole show was heavy, you know, tomelike. The scale of the show was enormous. When the Leader sang "The House at the Top of the Hill," she really *was* at the top of a hill. There was nothing expressionistic about the design. It was all very literal.

KANDER: There was a national touring company of Hal's production and we had the chance to do some revisions, and then Chita played the dark lady who we called the Leader. Those changes made a world of difference.

EBB: But the guiding conception came from Hal. I know

that when we wrote "Life is what you do while you're waiting to die," he loved how brazen it was. When we did the revival, there was a major issue about how we could no longer do the song because it was too dark. But we had done it that way, and I don't remember anybody getting up in the opening number and walking out, saying, "Hey, I'm depressed. I don't want to hear this." But I was pressured into changing the line. Even Joe Stein, who wrote the book, turned on me, saying, "It puts the audience in the wrong frame of mind."

KANDER: You know who else didn't like it was Sheldon Harnick.

EBB: And we heard Arthur Laurents didn't like it either. We had quite a few bright people who we respected saying, "For God's sake, change it." So I wrote, "Life is what you do till the moment you die." Which is softer. I always hated myself for that. I'm sorry I didn't dig in my heels and say no.

KANDER: We were both against it. We needed a Hal on the revival. Cacoyannis wanted to make sure that he did everything differently than Hal did.

EBB: I don't think Cacoyannis gave a hoot about anything. I never understood his opening in the revival. It rained up there for some reason.

KANDER: To give a big entrance for Quinn.

EBB: But Cacoyannis changed the opening in such a way that the song seemed irrelevant, whereas originally the song was the backbone of the philosophy of the show. Which was not ours but was Kazantzakis's—"Life is what you do while you're waiting to die." That was what Zorba was saying. "The world's a life sentence, you were born an imbecile." In many of our shows, the script has called for some statement of what life is. When I write the lyrics for a number like that, I don't have to agree with the song I've written. The song doesn't have to express my philosophy at all, but it does have to be the philosophy of the character who sings it. That opening song in *Zorba* was "Life Is." *Cabaret* contains those same two words. The philosophies of the two songs couldn't be more different, but the characters are also totally different:

Life is what you do while you're waiting to die.
Life is how the time goes by.
Life is where you wait while you're waiting to leave.
Life is where you grin and grieve.

Having if you're lucky, wanting if you're not.
Looking for the ruby underneath the rot.
Hungry for the pilaf in someone else's pot.
But that's the only choice you've got!

Life is where you stand just before you are flat.
Life is only that, Mister.
Life is simply that, Mister,
That and nothing more than that.

Life is what you feel till you can't feel at all.
Life is where you fly and fall.

Running for the shelter naked in the snow.
Learning that a tear drops anywhere you go.
Finding it's the mud that makes the roses grow.
But that's the only choice you know.

Wait!
Once again.

Life is what you do while you're waiting to die.
This is how the time goes by.

Harold Prince on *Zorba*:

I think *Zorba* is something of a masterwork, I always did. They did a revival with Tony Quinn, I have to tell you I didn't care for it. I think they compromised a lot of stuff but, God help us, they did make some money, which they didn't make in our version. I think our version suffered from two things. One, its opening number was unconventionally dark. It remains one of the best opening numbers I've ever heard. Two, we made the critical mistake of casting the leads with two people who had played opposite each other in *Fiddler on the Roof*, and so it tended to make it seem like a Greek version of *Fiddler on the Roof*. The project was brought to me by Herschel Bernardi, who had been Tevye in *Fiddler*. Now he wanted to play Zorba, and he was wonderful. It's just that I think people decided, "Oh, it's a lesser *Fiddler*." I think it's amazing, and, parenthetically, I read a lot of mail that has been collecting over forty years and has been put in books for me to see, and there's a whole section on *Zorba*, which is extraordinary because it is letters of praise from the damnedest people saying this is a masterwork. So that's why I chose the word. I was very proud of it.

KANDER: Working on the revival was terribly frustrating because there was a kind of allegiance between Anthony Quinn and Cacoyannis. It was hard to get through to them, and Cacoyannis had a difficult time communicating with the rest of the cast.

EBB: He never made anything clear to the actors. I think he liked us, and personally I liked him. But I thought he was a little volatile and hard to reach. It was my observation cast members had a lot of trouble with him.

KANDER: Anthony Quinn had a problem that would have

been comic if it weren't for the fact that you had to deal with it all the time. Anthony Quinn was rhythm-deaf the way some people are tone-deaf. But he had seen the movie so often that he really believed he could dance, and the fact is from the waist down that's not Quinn in the movie. But like people who believe their own publicity, he thought of himself as someone who could dance.

EBB: It was him saying, "I can do anything." Unlike someone like Lauren Bacall, who said what she couldn't do: "I cannot sing in that range and won't be able to deliver that song." Quinn, on the other hand, would say, "Choreograph me. Give me anything."

KANDER: Sure, why wouldn't he? He looks at the movie and says, "Boy, I'm really dancing up a storm." It was difficult to conduct because of his rhythm problems. We had to orchestrate little safety measures in the score so when he would not feel it rhythmically, he could get through it.

EBB: I don't believe he ever did anything musical before that show.

KANDER: But he did quite a lot of stage work. He was a real stage actor. Graciela Daniele had to choreograph for him. The famous Zorba dance. When you are choreographing for someone who can't count and has no sense of rhythm, it's nearly impossible. It came down to something so primitive in the song "The First Time."

EBB: His opening number.

KANDER: [*singing*] "I sniff at a woman . . ." Da, da, da— da, da, da.

EBB: He didn't know when to come in.

KANDER: So we finally had to have the chorus sing, "I sniff at a woman," and then count out loud, "One, two, three . . ."

EBB: But I tell you, outside of that, he was perfect in that part.

KANDER: Oh, he was fabulous. He really believed that was who he was.

EBB: He was Zorba. Zorba who had no rhythm. I think actors who came head-to-head with him had some difficulty because he could be a bully at times. The guy who played Nikos—who has practically nothing in the show but scenes with Zorba—had his problems with Quinn.

KANDER: Quinn thought he was lovable. Zorba is lovable, and I am Anthony Quinn and I am Zorba, therefore I am lovable.

EBB: He had a problem thinking that anybody could disagree with him.

KANDER: If I have the story right, the guy who was playing Nikos quit.

EBB: Robert Westenberg.

KANDER: Robert gave himself a Christmas present that year by quitting. As I remember him describing it, he went to Quinn and became rather ferocious. "You want me to love you? I can't love you! You're not lovable!"

EBB: Half the company was listening at the door because they wanted to hear him get ahold of Quinn. Basically, he was saying, "I can't act this part because there's no reality in it for me. I don't care about you the way Nikos should care about Zorba." It was too bad we had to lose Robert because he was a fine actor.

KANDER: I thought Quinn was terrific in the show. His curtain call was breathtaking.

EBB: Astonishing, and he did it every night. You would pay just to watch him take a curtain call. He held a flower and he came from all the way upstage peaking from behind the balustrade, like *Mourning Becomes Electra*, peeking out, as if to say, "Do you want me to come forward?" Of course they were cheering on their feet, and he would take that flower and walk slowly, humbly up to the apron of the stage, then stand there

with the flower, and just bow slightly. Then you knew he was going to throw that flower, and every woman in the audience
wanted to get it.

KANDER: Middle-aged women wet themselves when he was
on. They really did.

EBB: And finally, he threw it. I'll always remember that,
Quinn bowing.

KANDER: There were elements in that performance which
were really stunning because they came from him.

EBB: It did wonderful business, and nobody walked out of
the theater disappointed in him.

KANDER: They adored him.

EBB: When you have that kind of power, you know it, and I
think he played for that.

•   ◦   •

70, Girls, 70 was a show that allowed Kander and Ebb to deal
with relatively light material one of the few times in their careers.
The songwriters have a special affection for this fanciful tale
about a group of elderly but spry New Yorkers who embark on a
life of crime. Ebb co-wrote the libretto with one of his pre-
Kander collaborators, Norman Martin. The cast included Mil-
dred Natwick, Lillian Roth, Lillian Hayman, and Hans Conried.
Overshadowed that season by Stephen Sondheim's *Follies*, the
show opened at the Broadhurst Theater on April 15, 1971, and
lasted only thirty-five performances, the shortest run of any Kander and Ebb musical.

•   ◦   •

KANDER: My memory is that every show we did only had to do
with whether we wanted to work with that material. We were
certainly aware of everything that was going on around us, but in

terms of our work, I don't remember us ever having a conversation in which we decided now is the time to deal with this subject.

EBB: The closest we ever came to that was with *70, Girls, 70*, when one week that year on the covers of *Time* and *Newsweek* there were stories about geriatrics. That seemed to be the outside world peeking in and saying, "Hey, this would be a good time to deal with that subject." I remember being conscious of that when I wrote the book. The story was about a group of elderly people and one feisty lady in particular who becomes a Robin Hood and forms a gang with her fellow inmates in an old folks' home, which was actually a rundown hotel. They robbed places like Bloomingdale's and gave the money to the elderly and to the home where they lived. At the end, the leading lady dies—

KANDER: And ends up sitting on the moon.

EBB: She teaches them about living life to the fullest every day, and the piece ends with them singing, "Life keeps happening ev'ry day / Say yes."

KANDER: That show didn't go very far. It was a very blue-collar, Off-Broadway, backyard piece that should not have been on Broadway, or at least not in a large theater.

EBB: We were duped into putting it on Broadway, our own fault. Ron Field, with whom I had a long relationship and for whom I felt great affection, decided to do it and talked us into making it a Broadway show. When we finally did go that route, he quit.

KANDER: He didn't want to deal with old people.

EBB: He said, "I can't come in every morning and see a lot of old people standing around scratching and farting."

KANDER: For a show that ran only three weeks, we had wonderful times with it. It was one of the few shows that I've ever gone to night after night. Usually, once a show opens, it's over for us.

EBB: I loved that show like a father loves his weakest child.

The score was audience-pleasing, but I had no idea how to beat the first twenty minutes of exposition. I wrote that very clumsily. To this day I don't know how to make those first twenty minutes work, and I wish I did because I'm still fond of that show. Our director was not so wonderful and couldn't help me.

KANDER: We started with Paul Aaron and ended up with Stanley Prager. They were okay. I don't think it was anybody's fault.

EBB: Paul couldn't get the show up in time, so we missed our opening night in Philadelphia. We opened on a Wednesday matinee, which was very peculiar.

KANDER: We had an extraordinary cast. Everybody but one kid, Tommy Breslin, was eligible for Social Security. Some of them were in their eighties.

EBB: One day one of the eighty-year-old men was sitting next to me watching the rehearsal of a musical number. "That's a swell number," he said to me. I said, "Well, you better get the hell up there. Aren't you in it?"

KANDER: David Burns was one of the greatest clowns in the world, and he actually died onstage while we were in Philadelphia. He did a scene in the last act, dropped to the floor, and got a laugh.

EBB: The premise of the scene was that these old people had committed these robberies, and with the cops coming they were frightened. So they were pretending to be infirm, acting like they had no notion of reality. Davey's eyeglasses were way down on his nose, and he was shuffling along.

KANDER: He had a line where he had to come up from behind a desk and go to the center of the stage to deliver it. It was a laugh line and got a big laugh, and then he went back and came out for another line—

EBB: And crumpled to the floor.

KANDER: Since the last time he had been out there he got a big laugh, when he crumpled, the audience howled.

EBB: They thought he was pretending he couldn't walk to throw off the cops.

KANDER: Davey was the perfect example of what the show was about. On that same day he died, we had a rehearsal. He was sitting on a side seat, and Lillian Roth was sitting in back of him. He had his hand up her skirt, saying, "Lillian, one quick schtup with me will straighten you right out." That night he was dead, having gotten a laugh. Talk about living your life right up until the end.

EBB: I remember speaking at his memorial and the only thing I could think to say was: "How perfect for him that the last sound he ever heard was laughter because he lived for that."

KANDER: At the memorial, Carol Channing told us a marvelous story about a scene when she and Davey were out of town with *Hello, Dolly*. Gower Champion had the whole cast assembled and was reading them the riot act in the most terrible way. Davey was standing behind Carol Channing and said, as only he could, "Carol, let me tell you about my vasectomy." That got her through the rest of the meeting.

EBB: A wonderful guy and very funny. Only never put your hands behind your back when Davey is coming—he'll open his fly and put his dick right in your hand. He did that all the time.

KANDER: The experience with that show was a real lesson. I'm eligible to be in that show now, but those people, who were mostly in their seventies, were so full of positive energy. There was a seventy-four-year-old tap dancer named Bobbie Tremaine, and she came to us and said, "Look, I know this show is going to run a long time, but after it closes, is it all right if I use some of the songs in my act?" These people really lived as if they were going to live forever. We heard from them for years with their cards and memories. I think they're all dead now.

EBB: Sometimes we write a piece that closely expresses our own philosophy. "Yes" was one of those songs in *70, Girls, 70*. It meant a great deal to me personally at the time because it really was very much how I felt and how you felt as far as its message:

Yes.
Say "Yes."
Life keeps happening ev'ry day.
Say "Yes."
When opportunities come your way
You can't start wondering what to say
You never win if you never play.
Say "Yes."
There's mink and marigold right outside
And long white Cadillacs you can ride
But nothing's gained if there's nothing tried.
Say "Yes."

Don't say "Why?" say "Why not?"
What lies beyond what is,
Is not.
So what?
Say "Yes."

Yes, I can.
Yes, I will.
Yes, I'll take a sip.
Yes, I'll touch.
Yes, of course.
Yes, how nice.
Yes, I'd happily thank you very much.
Yes.
Oh, yes.
There's lots of chaff but there's lots of wheat.
Say "Yes."

Yes! Yes!
You might get mugged as you walk the street
But on the other hand, you might greet
That handsome stranger you've longed to meet.
Say "Yes."
Yes!

Don't say "Why?" say "Why not?"
What lies beyond what is,
Is not.
So what?

You can't look back on a chance that's lost.
Say "Yes."
Yes!
The dice mean nothing unless they're tossed.
The throw is usually worth the cost.
The hope of summer denies the frost.
Say "Yes."

Yes, I am.
Yes, I'll be.
Yes, I'll go.
Oh yes!
Yes!

EBB: What's life-affirming about our work, when that survival theme is there, stems from the story and the characters' need to affirm life, to go on, to be brave. We don't impose that. It's there in the material and we translate it in some way, as in that song.

KANDER: We'll never get to the end of this conversation, but there is an area in which we agree in terms of what we tend instinctively to want to work on, our taste and choice of material. I know in my case, to get psychological, it comes from the fact that I was brought up with the idea that things are supposed to be all right. If life is terrible, that's unnatural. I'm paraphrasing my folks and they would hate to sound like this. But the natural way of things by implication is that the good stuff is just around the corner waiting, and that's where you are supposed to be heading.

EBB: I'm nowhere near that, to my way of thinking.

KANDER: But you have the same attitude—

EBB: I like to believe that, but it certainly didn't come from my family upbringing. No one in my family ever encouraged me to believe that.

KANDER: But you focus on the idea of surviving so things will get better.

EBB: You have to. Doesn't everybody want to survive? At the end of *70, Girls, 70*, if a lady who is dead comes back to encourage her old friends to go on with their lives, why wouldn't she say yes? That comes right out of the needs of that plot. Personally, I also happen to believe in that survival theme. Come to the cabaret and make the most of it. If you look at our shows, there's a statement like that in most of them. Things are funny; things are tough; things are sad; but we survive.

KANDER: You may disagree with me, Freddy, but I think that is something that you may comment about in retrospect, but I don't ever remember us having a conversation and saying, "This is a show about survival so we're going to do it."

EBB: We don't go into a project thinking that.

KANDER: It just so happens that it is a theme that runs through our shows.

EBB: And whenever we can find that thread in a show we're writing, it's heartening.

KANDER: But it wasn't consciously there at the beginning.

EBB: You don't look for it, but you find it. It's fortuitous.

KANDER: I think we're both probably attracted to that kind of material. It may be a spiritual longing or belief that we share. At the end of *Kiss of the Spider Woman*, after these terrible things have happened to the window dresser, Molina, he actually becomes a movie star at least for a split second. That ending really moves me, that somehow some spirit of life is still there. Even Molina has his way of surviving before he dies.

EBB: But we didn't write that or think of that. That was the material, and luckily we were able to relate to it and translate it.

KANDER: A case where that spirit is not there is the end of *Cabaret*.

EBB: "Life Is a Cabaret" is not a happy song, given the context and what the song is really saying in that show. The audience now accepts it as entertainment, and if it gives people pleasure, that's fine. I think the song has taken on a life of its own. In the same way that you can't control your children, you have to let your songs go where they will.

KANDER: It is a very sad and dramatic song. The fact is that it is a song about a woman who has decided to have an abortion:

What good is sitting alone in your room?
Come hear the music play.
Life is a cabaret, old chum,
Come to the cabaret.

Put down the knitting, the book and the broom.
Time for a holiday.
Life is a cabaret, old chum,
Come to the cabaret.

Come taste the wine,
Come hear the band.

Come blow a horn, start celebrating:
Right this way, your table's waiting.

No use permitting some prophet of doom
To wipe every smile a-way.
Life is a cabaret, old chum,
Come to the cabaret!

I used to have a girlfriend known as Elsie.
With whom I shared four sordid rooms in Chelsea.
She wasn't what you'd call a blushing flower.
As a matter of fact, she rented by the hour.

The day she died the neighbors came to snicker:
"Well, that's what comes of too much pills and liquor."
But when I saw her laid out like a queen,
She was the happiest corpse I'd ever seen.
I think of Elsie to this very day.
I remember how she'd turn to me and say:

"What good is sitting alone in your room?
Come hear the music play.
Life is a cabaret, old chum,
Come to the cabaret.

Put down the knitting, the book and the broom,
Time for a holiday.
Life is a cabaret, old chum,
Come to the cabaret."

And as for me, as for me,
I made my mind up, back in Chelsea,
When I go I'm going like Elsie.

Start by admitting, from cradle to tomb
Isn't that long a stay.
Life is a cabaret, old chum,
Only a cabaret, old chum,
And I love a cabaret!

KANDER: Outside of our own collaboration, I think we always try to be open and flexible with our other collaborators. We like to work that way and we were taught to work that way by Mr. Abbott and by Hal. If there were one small point I would hope to make in this book, it is that none of the projects that we do, or that anybody worth his salt does in this business, are entered into frivolously with the idea of making a quick buck, as critics sometimes suggest. There isn't anyone we know writing in this area who doesn't approach the work very seriously with some sense of devotion and integrity. Sometimes you fuck it up and sometimes you don't. But it's never with that mercenary motive that you see implied in reviews that sound like "Oh, they were selling out" or "They were trying to cash in." That's just not true. Much of the work is much too arduous and demanding for that.

EBB: That sounds right to me. Musical theater is such a bastard art. Look at how many people come to bear on one number a lyric writer, a composer, a director, a librettist. To think of how many people can defeat a number—a bad horn player, a conductor getting a tempo wrong, a director not understanding it, a librettist not properly leading the audience into it, a performer who goes flat-footed or forgets a line. It's an amazing collaborative process, and the fact that anything comes off is quite remarkable considering how many elements have to conspire to make a number or a show work. The critics really hated *70, Girls, 70* and I've never quite understood why. It was one of the only times Stephen Sondheim ever complimented me. He had seen a matinee. I was in the back of the theater and as he was leaving, he called my name. I went over and said, "Hi, Stephen," and he said, "This is the best audience show I've seen in years. Everybody loves it. Congratulations." Jesus, I was thrilled!

KANDER: It was a strong audience show up until we opened.

EBB: It never occurred to me that the audience would hate it, until Sondheim's *Follies* opened, which was about three weeks before us. I went to the opening night with Carl and Joan Fisher, and I thought that show was just breathtakingly brilliant. At the end, I jumped up like everybody else. But then it occurred to me that show was also about getting old and dealing with it and having an affirmation. I wondered if that would hurt us. I mean, they were Tiffany's and we were Woolworth's. Then I became convinced in my own deeply neurotic way that, of course, it would kill us.

KANDER: And it did.

EBB: But, you know, it doesn't matter. The fact is you write 'em and you call 'em as you see them and hope for the best. And what else can you do?

KANDER: We've scarcely been mistreated, Freddy.

EBB: Oh, I never said that and certainly don't mean that. I think we've been treated very well, or else, after something like *70, Girls, 70*, how do you get your next one? After success, it's obvious how you get the next show, but after the failures, you have to wonder.

KANDER: The next one was *Chicago*.

● ◦ ●

While continuing their Broadway collaborations, Kander and Ebb also undertook a number of projects for television and film. Following the release of the movie *Cabaret* in February 1972, Ebb wrote Liza Minnelli's television special, *Liza with a Z*. Ebb and Bob Fosse produced the show while Ebb and Kander wrote songs. The production was filmed at Broadway's Lyceum Theater on May 31, 1972, for an invited black-tie audience. *Liza with a Z* was broadcast in September of that year and won an Emmy for Outstanding Single Program. The show's soundtrack spent more than five months on the charts.

The following year Ebb wrote and produced Frank Sinatra's television special *Ol' Blue Eyes Is Back*, with guest star Gene Kelly welcoming Sinatra out of a brief retirement. Turning again to movies, Kander and Ebb wrote several songs for the Barbra Streisand film *Funny Lady*, directed by Herb Ross. The movie was released in March 1975, with the Kander and Ebb song "How Lucky Can You Get?" earning an Oscar nomination. The duo went on to contribute songs to three Liza Minnelli movies: *Lucky Lady* (1975), *A Matter of Time* (1976), and *New York, New York* (1977). "The Theme from *New York, New York*" became an enduring hit for Frank Sinatra in 1980 and the official anthem of New York City.

● ● ●

E B B : I first worked with Frank Sinatra when I wrote his TV special *Ol' Blue Eyes Is Back*. Meeting him was kind of terrifying. Frank Loesser once told me en passant, "Don't ever meet your heroes. Chances are it will be a very disillusioning experience." And with Sinatra in many ways it was. I almost wish I didn't see what I saw or hear what I heard. I admired him enormously as a singer, but then I kept seeing him as a human being, and that was upsetting. I saw him snap his fingers to call one of his entourage to shine his shoes. I saw him be extremely cruel to Gene Kelly. All I can say about something like that is how disturbing it was.

Actually, Frank had wanted Redd Foxx to be the guest star on this show, the black comedian who was hilariously funny in the sitcom *Sanford and Son*. But I said to Frank, "I have no idea how to write for him. I don't know anything about Redd Foxx. I'm more at home with musical personalities, and I would very much like the guest to be Gene Kelly." Frank allowed that to happen, but he was not happy about it at any time, and I honestly don't know why. Frank used to call him "Shanty." That was his nickname for Gene, and I thought that was a little belittling right there. But Gene didn't seem to mind. He was the sweetest man, always humble and gracious.

I had to write the whole special and I used some numbers that Frank had done previously like "Free and Easy," during which Gene was to tap dance. Frank was not ungracious with me, though he would snap his fingers to call me too. "Fred," he would say, pointing to the script, "I don't want to say this." The script was based anecdotally on stories he told me. For instance, at one point in his movie career he was working with a leading lady, Michèle Morgan, in a movie called *Higher and Higher*. She was taller than he was, and the director made him stand on a box to play a love scene with her. I repeated that story in the script because I thought it was charming, but Frank refused to include it in the show. He called me over and said, "I don't want this in the script." So I had to take it out and we were left with holes in the show that he created because he actually didn't read the script until the day of the taping.

KANDER: What did we write for that show? Do you remember?

EBB: We wrote "We Can't Do That Anymore."

KANDER: Oh, that's right.

EBB: I thought it was a decent number, and Gene loved it. We were trying to be witty, saying now that we're over a certain age, we're still able to dance like the wind and coo like doves. Frank sang the line "I can't sing anymore," but he then proceeded to show you how well he did sing. Kelly sang, "I can't dance anymore," and then proceeded to show you how well he did dance.

ABOVE: Harold Prince (left), George Abbott, Liza Minnelli, Bob Dishy, Fred Ebb, and John Kander (at piano) working on *Flora, the Red Menace*, 1965 (Courtesy John Kander)

Fred Ebb, John Kander (at piano), and Jill Haworth as Sally Bowles rehearsing *Cabaret*, 1966 (Photofest)

Fred Ebb (left), John Kander, Barbra Streisand, Hal Prince, and Joe Masteroff at the Tony Awards, 1967. Streisand presented Kander and Ebb with their first Tony for the score of *Cabaret*. (Courtesy Fred Ebb)

Judi Dench as Sally Bowles in the first London production of *Cabaret*, 1968 (Photofest)

Liza Minnelli as Sally Bowles
in the 1972 movie of *Cabaret*
(Photofest)

Joel Grey (and chorus girl)
in the original Broadway
production of *Cabaret*, 1967
(Photofest)

BELOW: Alan Cumming as the
Emcee in the 1998 Broadway
revival of *Cabaret* (Photofest)

Robert Goulet as
Uncle Jacques in
The Happy Time,
1968 (Photofest)

Anthony Quinn in
the 1983 revival of
Zorba (Photofest)

Chita Rivera as Velma Kelly and Gwen Verdon as Roxie Hart in the original production of *Chicago*, 1975 (Photofest)

Gwen Verdon as Roxie and Jerry Orbach as Billy Flynn in *Chicago*, 1975 (Photofest)

Liza Minnelli in *The Act*, 1977 (Photofest)

Lauren Bacall (center) with cast members of *Woman of the Year*, 1981 (Photofest)

Bacall won a Tony for her performance in *Woman of the Year*, 1981. (Photofest)

Chita Rivera (left) and Liza Minnelli in *The Rink*, 1984 (Photofest)

Liza Minnelli (left) and Chita Rivera rehearsing *The Rink*, 1984 (Photofest)

Chita Rivera in *Kiss of the Spider Woman*, 1993 (Photofest)

Chita Rivera in *Kiss of the Spider Woman*, 1993 (Photofest)

Karen Ziemba (center), Daniel McDonald, and cast performing "Leave the World Behind" in *Steel Pier*, 1997 (Photofest)

Catherine Zeta-Jones and ensemble in *Chicago* (Photofest)

Catherine Zeta-Jones in the film version of *Chicago*, 2002 (Photofest)

BELOW: Renée Zellweger and Queen Latifah in *Chicago* (Photofest)

John Kander (left), Kaye
Ballard, Fred Ebb, and
Gwen Verdon, circa 2000
(Anita and Steve Shevett)

Chita Rivera (left),
Fred Ebb, Gwen
Verdon, and John
Kander, circa 2000
(Anita and Steve Shevett)

John Kander (left),
Debra Monk, and
Fred Ebb, circa 2000
(Anita and Steve Shevett)

It was not a bad number for the two of them. Frank learned it, and Gene learned it. But comes the night of the pre-record, Frank called me over before the taping and said, "I'm not recording that song." I said, "Why?" He said, "I've turned on it. I don't like it, and I don't want to do a number like that with Gene."

Gene Kelly was sitting in the control room. Frank said it to me on the floor, and I looked over at the recording booth. I saw Gene sitting there, and I don't know if he knew exactly what Frank was talking about, but there were gestures in his direction that would have given him a clue. I found that heartbreaking, and then the recording session started. Having not heard Frank say that he wouldn't record the number, the engineer said, "Frank, we'd like to set up for 'We Can't Do That Anymore.' Gene, are you ready?" Gene said, "Oh yes, I'm ready." Frank didn't say a word. Gene walked out of the booth and sang the song with him. They went on and recorded it, and I sat there open-mouthed. What did that mean? It seemed like Frank was throwing around his weight arbitrarily when it suited him, for whatever purpose people do things like that.

KANDER: There's a funny thing—this is just my opinion and I hope that I'm not being too harsh—

EBB: Oh, go on. I like when you're harsh.

KANDER: Something happens with people who become superstars. Their singing becomes no longer about the music that they're singing; it becomes more about them. So sometimes if you listen to a singer early in his or her career, you really hear very interesting songs, that is, the songs are illuminated. But more and more as they grow older and become more superstarrish and powerful, the singing is more about them singing, so that everything begins to sound the same.

EBB: I don't know how somebody of that kind of enormous stature can handle it without stooping to some kind of bullying tactic.

KANDER: But there are people who don't.

EBB: Oh, I know, but I mean they are superstars and they need to because of their own insecurities. They need some affirmation of that status.

KANDER: I don't know that people who are abusive should be forgiven just because they're insecure.

EBB: They don't know any other way.

KANDER: I think you're right, but it doesn't make me any more sympathetic toward them.

EBB: I'm not sympathetic to Frank or I wouldn't have told you the story, but I'm still in awe of him. The night we recorded the show, I had the opportunity to meet Lucille Ball and Fred Astaire, and Frank afforded me another thrilling moment in my life. I'm not grateful to him for the job. I wasn't paid any incredible sum of money, but I was grateful for the atmosphere and for meeting my own particular needs, which also include affirmation every five minutes. You didn't come to the taping?

KANDER: I didn't want to be there.

EBB: That was in California.

KANDER: As opposed to you saying that you were thrilled meeting all those people, I don't like to meet those people. I become my least comfortable self in that kind of social situation. It's not their fault. It's something I'm not good at. Just to cap your Sinatra story, his recording of "New York, New York" benefited us enormously and we are extremely grateful. But they had to rearrange the song because he didn't have the range to sing it. So there's a funny kind of transposition in it that makes you feel that he is going up, but in fact he is not. He also made lyrical errors. I watched him do it on television as a matter of fact, and he made the errors, I'm sure, because he forgot the lyrics. I've seen this happen with other people too. If you believe that you are a superstar and you make a mistake, you come to believe that your mistake must be better than the original because you're a superstar.

EBB: [*laughing*] You are the real cynic, and I write the lyrics. In that case, Frank did kill the rhyme.

KANDER: That was a huge hit, God knows, and we're very lucky to have had it. But he was not singing what you wrote.

EBB: Yes, I never wrote the line, "I'm A-number-one."

KANDER: It was something he had to make up on the spot when he couldn't remember the lyric. Then he became accustomed to singing it that way.

EBB: It stayed in his rendition of the number, and I never mentioned it. Frank called me when the song looked like it was going to break, and he said, "Well, we really did it, didn't we?" I almost said, "Well, now that you're my co-writer!" But you have to forbear with all of that—it doesn't do you any good. As you say, we're just very grateful for the exposure he gave that song.

KANDER: I've known major talents who are very straightforward and objective about what they are doing in their work. But there are others who buy into their own images.

EBB: It's an abuse of power, and it happens.

KANDER: I don't think they get better artistically during those periods in their lives. Imagine a serious singer—an opera singer or a lieder singer—saying, "Well, I just made this mistake in Brahms, so clearly it's an improvement." Betty Comden, Adolph Green, and Leonard Bernstein wrote a cabaret piece called "The Girl with Two Left Feet" that illustrates that type of attitude. The premise of the piece was that in front of Grauman's Chinese Theater there is an empty sidewalk block waiting for a star to put footprints in it, and one morning two left footprints are discovered in the block. Then there is a nationwide search for the girl with two left feet, because only stars have their footprints in front of Grauman's Chinese Theater, so obviously the girl who left the footprints must be a star. That's the same mentality you tend to see when a star comes to believe anything he or she does in performance, even a mistake, must be an improvement.

EBB: Interestingly enough, Liza also has that huge star status, but when she makes a mistake, she is contrition itself. She comes off the stage and says, "Oh, my God, I didn't get that right!" By the way, I don't understand that two-left-feet story.

KANDER: Forget it. But that's true about Liza. Even with all her problems, she is never abusive to anyone.

EBB: There's not a mean bone in her body.

KANDER: But some of her competitors are mean about her.

EBB: Even today the press is mean about her.

KANDER: The thing about Liza is this: the only person she is mean to is herself. I've never seen her deliberately want to hurt somebody.

EBB: I've never seen her lash out or anything like that.

KANDER: And she's had occasions where she could have.

EBB: Where she had cause. For all the problems she has had, she has managed to maintain her dignity and she is, after all, a very gracious woman. We wrote a lot of songs for her, and it was great to have a voice we could always count on. Other people perform songs of ours that Liza introduced, but Liza is Liza and nobody ever sang them like her. I think that about "New York, New York." As grateful as you are to Frank, it's Liza that you want to hear sing it. Not only as opposed to Frank but as opposed to anybody.

KANDER: I always felt it was a much more elegant song with her.

EBB: I think that derives from the respect that she has for music. Maybe she got that from her mother. Liza probably has more innate respect for songwriting and lyrics than anybody else.

KANDER: That's true.

EBB: Frank seemed to feel free to do what he did, which was to screw around, not only with Kander and Ebb, but with Cole Porter, with Irving Berlin. He murdered everybody's lyrics. Apparently, he sang whatever came into his head. Liza doesn't do that.

KANDER: If she has a change or something to suggest, she literally raises her hand: "Can I say something?" With Liza, it's about the music. She loves music. She loves jazz.

EBB: She loves words.

KANDER: She hears wonderfully.

EBB: I think that comes from what she heard her whole life with her mother.

KANDER: At a recording session, listening to an orchestra, she will hear things sometimes that I hadn't heard, and she will say in the most polite way, "Can we bring up the oboe?" It's never a frivolous suggestion. It's never a star suggestion. It's always really musical. She has real ears.

EBB: Whatever it is, you're grateful it's there and you get to hear your music sung by someone like that.

KANDER: Both Liza and Hal have played large parts in our careers, but in entirely different ways. Hal, besides giving us opportunities, was similar to Mr. Abbott in the sense of being an instructor and influencing our way of looking at the theater. He didn't intend it that way, but we watched how he directed and the way his mind worked.

EBB: In many ways, Hal invented us.

KANDER: Liza, to a certain extent for a long period of time, was our voice more than anything else. But I don't think Liza influenced us per se as songwriters.

EBB: I think of it as a liquid. In a way, Hal filled the container, but the liquid was Liza. It was sort of like a coffee maker. Hal was the grounds, Liza was the water, and out came us.

Liza Minnelli on Kander, Ebb, and Prince:

I might look at it differently. Hal may have been the grounds, but Fred and John were the blended coffee, and I just came out as what people liked to drink.

EBB: Hal certainly shaped our sensibilities, and Liza was the vehicle for how we expressed ourselves.

KANDER: Except Liza is not a Hal Prince kind of product in any way.

EBB: Oh no.

KANDER: The things that Hal represents in our lives are not the things that went into our relationship with Liza. Initially, you were her Pygmalion in the sense that you were most responsible for shaping her performance style. We did a television show with Liza once, and before she came on, I remember you sang "Liza with a Z." I realized watching you then that virtually every mannerism that people associated with Liza had come from you. I think her feelings for you in spite of the complications with the relationship are the best part of Liza. I don't know how to say this right. It's a healthy side of Liza that makes sense.

Liza Minnelli on Fred Ebb's influence:

Freddy was an amazing performer. He taught me what to say, he taught me how to move my hands, he taught me my delivery—he taught me everything. Where do you think I get these hands from? I bit my nails when I first started, and I couldn't do what everybody else did with their hands. I hated all of that. But when Fred performed, he was right up there and out front in a way that I thought, *Oh, I don't have to show my nails if I do it that way.*

EBB: She loved to have me perform things for her full out, and I loved doing that for her.

KANDER: She once said, "Sometimes I think I'm a figment of Fred Ebb's imagination." I think that is in a way absolutely true.

EBB: I loved her, and what came out of our relationship with her was a terrific rendition of what we did, one that was absolutely true to what we intended because she did it the way we wrote it and performed it the way we hoped to see it performed.

KANDER: Barbra Streisand was one who would change the music of a song.

EBB: But she didn't change lyrics. I think in order to really like Barbra, you have to diligently remind yourself of the humble background from which she sprang, how difficult it must have been for her, how needy she was of the stardom that she attained. I looked at her with enormous sympathy with the particular experience that we had doing the movie *Funny Lady*. I heard a funny story about Barbra and the producer of *Funny Lady*, whose name was Ray Stark. It went like this. Ray presented Barbra with a horse. She recently had bought a ranch, and he gave her a horse. About two days later, she came in *wild* because her horse died, and it seemed to be her unshakable conviction that Ray had given her a sick horse on purpose. And now she had to bear the pain of losing the animal. There was something else I remember. As you know, when I'm fortunate enough to get them, I collect Egon Schiele's work. I saw a gorgeous Schiele on Barbra's wall and coveted it at once. I said, "My God, what a great painting! I'll write this movie for nothing but the painting." But she said, "Nothing doing! Stark gave it to me." Apparently, Ray was in the habit of giving her lavish presents. Imagine, a Schiele and a horse!

KANDER: I'll always remember that other story. Remember the white rug?

EBB: On the white rug under her piano, there was doggy-doo the night when we played the score at her house. She had a house at the time near mine in Holmby Hills.

KANDER: It wouldn't be funny except for the fact that her house was so immaculate, and every once in a while as you walked from room to room you almost expected there to be a price tag on some objet d'art. She was actually for the most part never unkind to us. My experience in the recording studio was just terribly frustrating. There was a song called "Isn't This Better?" that we wrote for her Fanny Brice character in the movie. What Barbra was singing with that number and what they were arranging were so far away from the song that I could hardly believe it. It soon became clear that I was unhappy, and I remember the musical director, Peter Matz, trying to calm me down. Finally, it boiled down to an exasperated Barbra saying, "Well, what did you write in the first place?" So I said, "This is what we wrote," and I played her the song. She said, "Oh, well, that's nice." Then she recorded the song the way we wrote it.

EBB: "Let's Hear It for Me"—wasn't that song another issue?

KANDER: That was an arrangement.

EBB: The accompaniment that they had invented was exactly the same as—

KANDER: The Jule Styne song—

EBB: "Don't Rain on My Parade," compounded by the fact that "Let's Hear It for Me" was staged in exactly the same way that "Don't Rain on My Parade" had been. There was Barbra on her way somewhere.

KANDER: I was so embarrassed by that. It amazed me that they let it happen. Later I ran into Jule Styne backstage at a show, and I said, "Jule, about that song." I started to explain, but he said, "I know you didn't do that." He knew exactly what had happened. There was only one time I remember Barbra saying something mean, and that wasn't directed at us. She had recorded our early songs "My Coloring Book" and "I Don't Care Much" on the same album. Later, Tommy Valando had us take a couple of new songs that we had written to her. She was backstage someplace.

EBB: At *Funny Girl*.

KANDER: We played the songs for her. We had, after all, known her before she was Funny Girl. She listened while she was making up, and she said basically that she wasn't interested. But she also said rather pointedly, "Why don't you give them to that Minnelli girl!"

EBB: Oh, I remember that. How nice that we remember the same thing. She did say that, and yet whenever she came to see Liza, she was always quite gracious.

KANDER: She was usually very gracious with us, too.

EBB: I thought so. Barbra never said or did anything unpleasant to me. Again, it was just my observation about her regard for the music, as it was with Frank.

KANDER: By way of observation, I don't think I'm very good with movies in general unless I am working with a director who is very encouraging. I've done some film work, both with you and on my own, and when it's fun, it's fun. But when it's part of a big corporation breathing down your neck, it's not fun, which is why I do so few movies. Years ago I started writing background music on a film, and the music director at the studio was overseeing the project. I backed out because I knew that he told one young composer, "If you're going to live here in Hollywood, I'll help you, but if you're going to live in New York, I'll see to it as much as I can that you don't work in this business."

EBB: With the movie of *Cabaret*, we wrote "Mein Herr" and "Money" in New York, and also added "Maybe This Time," which we had written earlier. Fosse took those songs with him when he went over to Europe to make the movie. You and I weren't invited. In movies, that's the way it works—we just write them and hope for the best.

KANDER: Very often when we work on a movie that way—when somebody says, "Would you write a song for us?"—we have almost no connection with the project.

EBB: It's like making a deposit at a bank. You just walk away and hope that they credit it to your account.

KANDER: With *Lucky Lady*, we just wrote the songs.

EBB: We didn't even have the script. Stanley Donen was the director and he told us on the phone what he wanted. "I would like a number for Liza, who plays a character in a seedy Mexican nightclub. What kind of number would she sing? I'd like a title song." Did we write one other song for that?

KANDER: Sure.

EBB: I remember "Get While the Gettin' Is Good."

KANDER: You and Liza and I performed "Lucky Lady" once, as a matter of fact, on some afternoon television show. I think it was the *Dinah Shore Show*.

EBB: We did? I don't remember that.

KANDER: That's my memory of it. I can sort of see us standing there, but maybe that's my imagination.

EBB: All I know is that Stanley asked us on the phone to write those songs, and as I remember they came very easily.

KANDER: They were fun to write but the movie wasn't great.

EBB: No. The ending was changed. The original ending was kind of grim. There were two characters played by Burt Reynolds and Gene Hackman. Liza was one corner of the triangle. At the end they both died and she was left alone on a beach. She was holding one of them in her arms and the other one came floating by.

KANDER: And there was a very slow reprise of one of the songs.

EBB: I remember it was contrapuntal. But they cut that ending and instead gave it a happy ending with Liza behind a steering wheel singing, "Bless my soul . . ." It was silly. The whole movie didn't do very well, but I enjoyed that assignment.

KANDER: We had no investment in it at all. Nobody was going to ask us how to make the movie. We just wrote the songs on assignment. Working on a movie, at least for me when I write background music, you really have to be working for only one person, and that has to be the director. You have to develop a relationship with that person. He has to help you find—or some-times you collaborate on finding—what the music needs to do in any given scene. But if I'm working for a committee of people, that scares me. I don't know how to do that. I would not know how to be a regular film writer. I worked with Robert Benton on *Kramer vs. Kramer* [1979], *Still of the Night* [1982], and *Places in the Heart* [1984], and he was terrific. We would look at a scene and he would say specifically, "I need music to tell me this, which the actors are not telling me or the script is not telling me." That's a great help, and he's a wonderfully talented man. But writing songs together as we did for a movie like *Lucky Lady* is a different process.

EBB: They weren't specifically character songs either.

KANDER: When I write background music, the process in-volves watching the movie several times with the director. Then I get a machine and watch it by myself. John Erman is somebody else who I've done several movies with, and the process with John is exactly the same. I sit with the director, and he may say, "Right here it needs something," and then we discuss it. Eventu-ally, once we've done that, he will give me a machine to take home, and I work on it there. There will be a mark on the film where the music is to start. That may be something that the two of us have decided together, and there will be another mark where we decided the music should disappear. It's like an old-time piano player playing for a silent film. That's fine if you have a director who is supportive and doesn't make you feel like you're untalented.

There was one movie with Meryl Streep, *Still of the Night*, and I remember writing the background music for that. It's funny, but I work on a film so intently and for so many hours that I re-ally come to think that I know the actress. I was later introduced to Meryl Streep, and because I had been looking at her so much, I thought, *She must know me*. The same thing happened with *An*

Early Frost [1985], which I did with John Erman. Aidan Quinn had the lead in it, and he lives up near me in the country. I worked on it so intently that when I finally met him, I thought, *I know him but he has no idea who I am.* Working on movies is a strange experience, but it can be fun. I loved doing *Breathing Lessons.* That was a charming movie based on a novel by Anne Tyler.

EBB: With Joanne Woodward. Awesome.

KANDER: That was John Erman directing again, and we worked through the same process with the machine. One thing in particular strikes me as fun that I have with a director as far as the music goes. I'm not a fan of movies where music is playing all the time, but if a scene has been written in such a way that the characters are saying one thing and the music is to tell you that's not what they're really thinking about, then you have a chance to do something that's more illuminating.

Freddy, you may think I'm too romantic about this, but I think that the theatrical community in New York is very small and much more close-knit compared to Hollywood. There isn't really as much of a sense of community in the movie business. In New York, there is a kind of support that comes just from being part of the community. The theater really is sort of classless—the stage manager, the head carpenter, and the star of the show are all family. It doesn't matter whether or not you're a success this year. You're accepted as a professional once you have proven yourself through your work. I sometimes think of it this way. In Hollywood they ask, "What are you doing now?" In New York they ask, "Who are you?"

EBB: I think that's right. I often do think you're too romantic with your views, but not about that. There's a totally different sense of community in the theater in New York. It's more like a family here. [*laughing*] Or maybe an asylum.

FIVE

Chicago on Broadway

Kander and Ebb worked with Bob Fosse again on *Chicago*, the sensational twenties tale of murder and vaudeville, loosely based on the 1926 play by Maurine Dallas Watkins. In addition to writing the lyrics, Ebb collaborated with Fosse on the book. With work on the musical barely under way, Fosse suffered a heart attack in November 1974. When he returned three months later to rehearse the show, he became increasingly abusive with his cast and collaborators. During the tryout run, Kander told Ebb, "No show is worth dying for. Let's go home."

But the songwriters persevered and stayed with the production. The cast included Fosse's wife, Gwen Verdon, as Roxie Hart, Chita Rivera as Velma Kelly, and Jerry Orbach as Billy Flynn. *Chicago* opened to mixed reviews on June 1, 1975, at the 46th Street Theater. Some critics found the show, with its crime-does-pay theme, too cynical. Though losing across the board at the Tonys that year to Michael Bennett's *A Chorus Line*, *Chicago* managed a run of 923 performances. Kander and Ebb scored memorably with "All That Jazz," "Razzle Dazzle," "My Own Best Friend," "Me and My Baby," "Cell Block Tango," and the heartrending "Mr. Cellophane." Bob Fosse's 1979 movie, *All That Jazz*, was based in part on his experiences bringing *Chicago* to the stage. Kander and Ebb begin their reminiscences by recalling how Fosse's movie distorted the personalities and actual events that took place while they were working on the show.

• ● •

EBB: I was initially offended by *All That Jazz*.

KANDER: I was too.

EBB: By Bob Fosse's depiction of the character who was the songwriter.

KANDER: Oh, I wasn't thinking about the songwriter.

EBB: Who people easily could have thought was based on me or you.

KANDER: No, I know who the character was based on, as a matter of fact, because Bobby told me. It was someone Bobby worked with long before he met us.

EBB: I knew too. But my fear was nobody else was going to know.

KANDER: The thing that offended me about the movie was this: it was all about Bobby pretending to be honest. He was saying, I'm not worth much, but everybody around me is worth even less. The fact is that he was ascribing motives and activities to people around him during the making of *Chicago* that simply were not so.

EBB: If you watch the movie carefully, Bobby is always the victim and that was not so in reality.

KANDER: He pretends to be confessing to his own failings, but it's a put-down of almost everybody else with the exception of Gwen Verdon. Everybody in the movie is portrayed as really trying to do terrible things behind Bobby's back. Do you think he really believed all of that?

EBB: Yes, I do. I think that Bobby had a classic victim complex. There are many in my experience, performers especially, who are constant victims—"I was a nice guy, *but* . . ." "I behaved beautifully, *but* . . ." It's always the other guy who's doing them in. I find that very disconcerting. It was fascinating with Bobby because he made up things out of whole cloth. I wasn't positive that was what he was doing until he called to interview me for the movie he was making. I was in California when Bobby called. He was very pleasant, very loving, first asking me, "Can I use the song title 'All That Jazz,' for the movie? Because it's yours." I said, "Actually, it's not. I was reading one of the *Time-Life* book series, and there was a chapter entitled 'All That Jazz.' I took it from there. I didn't really invent it, Bob." He was impressed with that and how I had always done that kind of thing ever since he had known me. He said, "If there is a line that you take from somebody, you acknowledge it. I never do. The sincerest form of flattery is to steal." He believed that, and when I look at the work he did, I can see that he often borrowed from other sources, vaudeville routines and so forth.

During our phone conversation, he used a tape recorder and proceeded to question me. I remember him asking, "When I had my heart attack during *Chicago*, when you knew that I wasn't going to be back for rehearsals for a while and that it might have meant closing down the show, what was your reaction?" I said, "I was horrified, Bob. I was disappointed and sad." Then he asked, "What about the rest of the people who were involved with the show? Was anybody happy?" I said, "No, nobody was happy."

KANDER: I never heard this story.

EBB: He said, "I thought people were happy. Gwen told me a couple of people were happy." I said, "Nobody was happy. It was the loss of a job if nothing else, and a concern for you, who we all clearly idolized. Why would we be happy?" Then he said, and this I remember distinctly, "Let's get off that. What about Hal Prince?" I said, "What about Hal Prince?" He said, "When you and Kander went to Hal Prince to have him take over the show . . ."

KANDER: What?

EBB: ". . . With Bobby Fryer and Marty Richards."

KANDER: *What!*

EBB: He said, "You apparently thought I was going to die." I said, "That never happened. We never went to Hal." But he insisted, "Well, somebody went to Hal Prince." I said, "I don't know who your sources are, Bobby, but if somebody went to Hal Prince, it was certainly not John, and it was certainly not me, and we certainly would not have approved of that. Nobody wanted to take the piece away from you. I mean, you wrote it with me and it was your idea from the beginning." The conversation went on and on like that.

KANDER: Obviously, he held on to the belief—

EBB: That he had been betrayed.

KANDER: That we wanted Hal to take over as director. In the first place, oddly enough, if we were going to go to somebody to take over that show, it would not have been Hal. He didn't like the material.

EBB: Hal never liked *Chicago*. He hated the show even when it was a hit. He thought we ripped off *Cabaret*. He wrote us a note saying that.

KANDER: One of his less temperate notes.

EBB: "Tell Bob Fosse that Chicago in the late 1920s is . . . not Berlin."

KANDER: "Not Berlin," right.

EBB: I remember that vividly.

KANDER: But this is interesting. Why in the face of not only denial but no proof would Fosse put it in the movie?

EBB: Because he wanted it there.

KANDER: Yes, but why would he cling to believing that?

EBB: Because it gave him pleasure to feel that he was being betrayed. He wanted to be the victim.

KANDER: So he really believed that?

EBB: Absolutely. He believed it.

KANDER: That's really sick.

EBB: Because we had already a long relationship with Hal,

if Bobby were to conjecture who we would go to, he would select Hal.

KANDER: So imagining makes it true.

EBB: Yes.

KANDER: When he came back after his heart attack, he got really dark. He was not that way as much before he was sick. He was much more fun when we first knew him. I think he had gone through a great deal with his heart bypass operation, and I think in some way that affected the work we did on the show. The show became more cynical and biting than it had started out to be. Bobby was a terrific man with a very dark side, and there was always something self-destructive about his behavior. But once we got into rehearsal, things became very unpleasant, not so much for me, but you had a terrible time. The atmosphere was not good, and he and Gwen were having a difficult time, too. At one point I remember she said, "They can pack his heart in sawdust as far as I'm concerned." But Gwen's feelings for Bobby were so complicated that it's very hard to know what the truth was from her vantage point.

EBB: In that same conversation I had with him, he said, "I know you must have thought while we were working on *Chicago* that I was picking on you." That was exactly what he said, and I told him, "Honestly, Bobby, yes, I did think that." He said, "Well, I *was* picking on you. Do you know why? Because you are vulnerable, and vulnerable people drive me crazy." As if that were enough of a reason! One of his scapegoats during *Chicago* was Michael Vita.

KANDER: Oh, God!

EBB: Michael Vita played the district attorney, and during the trial scene he had only two words to deliver: "Your witness." After that line, Billy Flynn would launch into his summation.

KANDER: I remember Bobby was horrible to Michael.

EBB: Poor Michael could not say "Your witness" the right

way. Bobby would do the line for him, "No, no! Yooooouuur . . . witness." Michael would dutifully say, "Yooooouuur . . . witness." It went on and on, and Bobby had the poor guy in tears. He simply could not say it the way that Bobby wanted. Two words. It was terribly frightening. I took Michael Vita out to dinner that night to try to console him. He was absolutely distraught.

KANDER: This may seem like a detour, but it's not. There is a long chapter about Kathleen Battle in the book *Molto Agitato*. Apparently, her behavior became more and more insulting to the people who she worked with, and eventually she was fired by the Metropolitan Opera. After those occasions when she was abusive to people onstage during rehearsals, her manager would always come back and say, "Well, you just don't understand her—she's a perfectionist." Isn't that a wonderful word? Most bullies like that will try to justify their behavior that way. If you caught them in mid-shriek or mid-insult when they were screaming at an actor, and if you asked why they were doing that, they would say, [*shouting*] "BECAUSE I WANT IT RIGHT!"

EBB: Oh, not so loud.

KANDER: That's exactly how scary it is when you confront them.

EBB: The thing is that seldom happens to them. Nobody does stop and say, "Hey, why are you doing that?" You just become more terrified, even as a spectator sitting there watching it happen. I don't know anybody who had the guts to go up to Bob Fosse and say, "Hey, why are you doing that?" He just did it. I remember Neil Simon was called in by Bobby to see the show. He was another guy who we heard Bobby felt had betrayed him because Neil Simon and his wife, Marsha Mason, gave shelter to Gwen during one of their marital altercations, and Bobby considered that really hostile. But Neil Simon and Marsha Mason came to see *Chicago*, and Bobby was talking to them at the end of the show, asking Neil if he would come in and add some jokes to pep the thing up or fix whatever he imagined was wrong with it.

KANDER: That was during previews. We were all onstage with the creative staff, and it was a humiliating moment for Bobby.

EBB: He and Neil went over and sat on the stairs to talk privately, and eventually Neil and Marsha left. You thought she and Neil didn't love the show, and you were right. When they left, I asked Bobby, "Is Neil going to help us?" Now, mind you, I didn't really think we needed all that much help, but Bobby did, so therefore we did. He said, "Oh no, Neil hated it. But don't feel bad." Neil Simon did not like the show and would not come in to help us.

KANDER: He was very public about it, Freddy. There was another incident that took place three or four days before we opened. Bobby had some really awful stuff that he was putting in the show and we kept wanting him to take it out. It was something really vulgar that distracted from the piece, and we went backstage with all our courage and asked him about it. He got very nasty. Then suddenly he said, "And by the way, why didn't you ever give me the rewrite on the 'Roxie' number?" You started to say, "But, Bobby!"

EBB: I said, "I didn't know you wanted a rewrite!" I was very upset at that point, and you took me by the shoulder, turned me around, and walked me straight out of the theater.

KANDER: Yes, I turned you around and said, "Good night," and we walked out the stage door. That was, believe it or not, something I had learned from Liza, a healthy thing that I learned from Liza. She told me a story about shooting the movie of *Cabaret*. At one point after she did a scene, Bobby demanded, "Liza, I want you to come into my office right away. I want to talk about this right now!" She said, "No, Bobby, we'll talk about it tomorrow because if I go in there now, you're going to say something to me and tomorrow you're going to send me flowers to apologize for it. So we'll talk about it tomorrow." Then she left. Now, whether that story is true or not, it was a real lesson for me, the idea that you don't have to play somebody else's script. That flashed in my head when I turned you around and we went out the door.

EBB: Liza had other devices, too. When she was on the brink of being yelled at by Otto Preminger during *Tell Me That You Love Me, Junie Moon*, she would cry. She would start bawling and suddenly be this pathetic little girl, and Preminger deferred. He wouldn't yell at her. So there were devices for putting people like that off. Unfortunately, I didn't know any of them.

KANDER: When you were in the midst of your agony with Fosse while we were in Philadelphia, I said to you, "Why don't we get on a train and go back to New York. This isn't worth it. No show is worth dying for. Let's go home."

EBB: Philadelphia was not good.

KANDER: I wasn't going through it as badly as you, but I remember lying on the bed in my hotel room and thinking, *I'm going to die here.*

EBB: I realize now that I was really the whipping boy. It was not only that I was the most vulnerable, but something else that he told me later. He said that he liked me the best. Maybe I suited some image of a whipping boy that was pleasant for him because I was malleable. I never stood up to him. I never argued with him. That was how the show was written. I would go home every night, write a scene, bring it in the next day, and show Bobby. He would say, "Oh, this is all right," but he was never very wholehearted in his praise. The mere fact that he accepted it was terrific as far as I was concerned. I revered him back then, and he did initially give me the courage to write the book. I also knew when I played a number for him and he approved it, that number was going to be terrific.

For all the difficulty working with him, and that was enormous, I always thought it was worth it. It's a very complicated issue, isn't it? There you are working with a man who in your opinion is a bona fide genius. But at the same time, he shows discernible signs of being a detestable bully. I can't imagine how other people would deal with that. I know what I have seen. I saw Herb Gardner and Paddy Chayevsky have lunch with him daily. They thought the world of him and yet were able to say to me, "Don't be afraid of him. He's an arrogant son of a bitch, but he knows what he is doing. Don't let him bully you. Stand up to him. You're every bit as talented as he is." I think what happened was that I made peace in my mind with all of the contradictions and allowed my own love of the work on *Chicago* to supersede everything.

KANDER: I remember that you were extremely enthusiastic from the start, and I was excited to work with Bobby and Gwen as well, but I was concerned at first that *Chicago* might be another piece that we were writing where show business would be a metaphor for life.

EBB: I was interested in the original play, *Chicago*. The film adaptation, *Roxie Hart*, starred Ginger Rogers, but the movie was of no use in writing the book. As I understood it, Bobby and Gwen always wanted to adapt the play *Chicago*, but they never figured out how to make it into a musical. Bobby and I were close after working on *Cabaret* and *Liza with a Z*, and one day he said to me, "Can't you find a way to make this *Chicago* material into a musical? Fred, I think you could write the book." When Bob Fosse said you could do something, you somehow felt you could do it. So I made it vaudeville based on the idea that the characters were performers. Every musical moment in the show was loosely modeled on someone else: Roxie was Helen Morgan, Velma was Texas Guinan, Billy Flynn was Ted Lewis, Mama Morton was Sophie Tucker.

KANDER: One of the reasons that we call *Chicago* a vaudeville is because many of the songs that we wrote are related to specific vaudeville performers like those you mentioned, and Eddie Cantor and Bert Williams as well. We listened to recordings by those people. Again, it was that unconscious process of listening to a lot of jazz from that period, letting your brain soak it in and then writing. To some people, this may sound like a crude way of doing research, but it works for me. I have this absolute confidence that the style of the music that we've been listening to seeps into our unconscious and comes out in our own language.

EBB: *Chicago* was an entertainment, but it also said something about celebrity, about our celebrating killers. At the time Squeaky Fromme of the Manson family was on the cover of *Time*, and that sort of infamy was initially what the show was about. I thought of it this way: ask most Americans who the secretary of state is, and they won't be able to tell you; but ask them who Al Capone is, and they will know right away.

KANDER: Life around the *Chicago* production was never pleasant. When we were out of town, the ending of the show had two songs in it for the girls, and they just didn't quite work, though we liked them.

EBB: Right. We had a finale in which Roxie and Velma come together to do their club act, and the act that we decided to do was a rather cheesy club act where Chita played the drums and Gwen played the saxophone. They sang a song called "It" and another called "Loopin' de Loop." They were very amusing, but mostly to us, the sight of Chita banging the drums—

KANDER: And Gwen honking on the saxophone. I remember we were rehearsing in a hotel ballroom. Fosse and Stuart Ostrow, who was assisting him, came to us much more politely than usual and said, "Would you mind going off and reconsidering the ending and writing another song for it?" They were terribly apologetic.

EBB: Bobby thought the girls should have a more sophisticated club act, so he wanted us to scotch those two songs and replace them with one song to accommodate the club act.

KANDER: We said we would try, reluctantly, with an attitude that we would do it just to be cooperative. I will always remember the face we put on for them. As we left, we didn't even look at each other. We went out the ballroom door and started skipping down the hallway, laughing gleefully.

EBB: It was like they gave us a vacation in Florida.

KANDER: We went out to where the piano was and wrote the song "Nowadays" in a very short time.

EBB: No more than an hour.

KANDER: We took the day off and then brought in the song so it would seem like we had done a lot of work to come up with the new number.

EBB: We spent the entire day away just to make it look hard, and then Bobby and Stuart liked the song, and it went into the show.

KANDER: I remember when we wrote "Razzle Dazzle," before we took it in and played it for Bob, you said with absolute confidence, "Try adding a couple of finger snaps to it. Bobby will love that." We added them, and then we took it in and played it for Bob, and as soon as he heard the finger snaps, he loved the song.

EBB: As I recall, "Cell Block Tango" was a very difficult number to write. It's not so much a song as a musical scene for six women, and each has to tell her personal story in the course of a musical refrain that keeps repeating. It was difficult because each of the stories had to be entertaining and also meaningful. Each one had to be of a length that didn't go on too long and run the risk of being boring. We kept rewriting and rewriting those stories that the women told to go with the refrain—

He had it coming
He had it coming
He only had himself to blame.

If you'd have been there
If you'd have seen it
I betcha would have done the same!

KANDER: When Gwen was sick during *Chicago*, Liza took over for eight weeks and she came close to making the show a hit.

EBB: She did all of Gwen's blocking.

KANDER: She learned that show in a week.

EBB: I guess I should confess this. I had been with Liza in California, and when we were on our way back to New York on the plane, when I knew Liza was going to do *Chicago*, I was egging her on to get little things back into the show that I lost during my collaboration with Fosse. I desperately wanted "My Own Best Friend" to be a song just for Roxie. That was the way it was originally supposed to be done. But Bobby took that song and added Chita as Velma. He had them at the edge of the stage, obviously mocking the high-end cabaret singers with their phony Oh-look-at-me attitude. He hated songs like—

KANDER: "I Did It My Way."

EBB: And "I Gotta Be Me." He hated them. And this was his take on how you would sing "My Own Best Friend" if you were that kind of performer. I thought what he did belittled the song. But Liza knew she had power coming into the show, and on the plane she told me, "I'll get it back." During a rehearsal, she said, "Bobby, I would like to sing this number by myself." That meant having Chita not come out, which was fine with Chita. The first night that Liza sang it, she got a tremendous hand, and she whispered into the microphone, "How about that, Bobby!" I don't know who heard her. To me it was like she had yelled it out.

KANDER: I never heard that.

EBB: I was frightened that she said it. "How about *that*, Bobby." But she idolized him. I remember when we did *Liza with a Z*, Bobby made "Ring Them Bells" a production number.

KANDER: "Ring Them Bells" had always worked reasonably

well, but it had never been staged like that. What Bobby did was breathtaking.

EBB: He did it wonderfully. Interestingly enough, after *Liza with a Z*, she was going on the road and she couldn't afford to take as many people with her in the *Liza with a Z* company. She had to call Bobby and ask him to restage the number for fewer people. It doesn't look as good with fewer people, but he was fine with it and very loving about it. He came to the studio in the morning about ten, and he had to go to East Hampton at exactly twelve-thirty because he was being picked up. So he was there two and a half hours. About a week later, Liza called me and said, "Bobby charged me twenty-five thousand dollars for restaging that number." I said, "Oh, really?" She said, "Yes, what should I do?" I said, "It's like that old line, pay the two dollars." Liza said, "Pay it!" I said, "What are you going to do, argue with him? No." She said, "Isn't that a lot of money?" I said, "Oh yeah!" He soaked her, but he got his money.

KANDER: During the *Chicago* run, there was no publicity for Liza replacing Gwen, no sign in front of the theater. Every night the stage manager would say, "Tonight the role of Roxie Hart, usually played by Miss Gwen Verdon, will be played by Liza Minnelli." We weren't doing well before Liza came into the show. Our reviews had been very mixed.

EBB: Oh, I think the show was going to close. Liza was the one who made it a hit, right?

KANDER: It wasn't really a hit. It never paid back. What happened was that people began thinking of the show as a hit with Liza, so when Gwen came back, business was good. That was Liza at her most amazing.

EBB: I remember Brooks Atkinson's review of *Chicago* basically said something like, "It is too slight a piece to sustain its atmosphere."

KANDER: Many critics thought it was just too mean.

EBB: Yes, sardonic wasn't in that year.

KANDER: Writing "Class" was fun in that way where we were able to just let go.

EBB: That was a duet for Velma and the prison matron. After we had written it, I remember having serious second thoughts about that number:

Velma:
What ever happened to fair dealing,
And pure ethics
And nice manners?
Why is it everyone now is a pain in the ass?
What ever happened to class?

Matron:
Class?
What ever happened to "Please, may I?"
And "Yes, thank you"?
And "How charming"?
Now every son of a bitch is a snake in the grass.
What ever happened to class?

Velma and Matron:
Class!
Ah, there ain't no gentlemen
To open up the doors.
There ain't no ladies now,
There's only pigs and whores,
And even kids'll knock you down
So's they can pass.
Nobody's got no class!

Velma:
What ever happened to old values?

Matron:
And fine morals?

Velma:
And good breeding?

Matron:
No one even says "oops"
When they're passing their gas. What ever happened to class?

Velma:
Class!

Velma and Matron:
Ah, there ain't no gentleman
That's fit for any use,
And any girl'd touch your privates
For a deuce.

Matron:
And even kids'll kick your shins and give ya sass.

Velma:
And even kids'll kick your shins and give ya sass.

Velma and Matron:
Nobody's got no class!

Velma:
All you read about today is rape and theft.

Matron:
Jesus Christ! Ain't there no decency left?

Velma and Matron:
Nobody's got no class.

Matron:
Everybody you watch

Velma:
S'got his brain in his crotch.

Matron:
Holy crap.

Velma:
Holy crap.

Matron:
What a shame.

Velma:
What a shame.

Velma and Matron:
What became of class?

EBB: I almost talked myself out of that one. Funny songs actually terrify me. I'm at a loss there because very seldom do I think what I've written is funny. I would have cut "Class" in two minutes from my own fear of it before I saw it on the stage. I know we often write comic songs that come off, but I never know whether a song will work while I am writing it. With "Class," we kept trying to find "ass" rhymes. I came up with "Last week my mother got groped in the middle of Mass!" I remember you laughed so hard when you heard that line you almost fell off the piano bench. We both loved the line, and Chita loved it. We put it in a matinee that same day, but there was dead silence from the audience. So we took the line out. I can be easily discouraged that way.

KANDER: I have more belief in your humor than you have.

EBB: But that's what gets me through. If you had not stuck with "Class," that number would have been out. I didn't even do it at the backers' audition. I thought it would bomb and refused to do it. The first night the song went into the show, I panicked. I ran downstairs to the men's room to hide. Eventually, I heard the audience laughing and decided to go back up. On the steps, I heard more laughter, and on the line "No one even says 'oops' when they're passing their gas," there was a really huge laugh. Only then did I realize the song was funny.

KANDER: My feeling about your humor, your humor lyrics if you want to call them that, is that if the audience doesn't get it, that doesn't necessarily mean it's not funny. Many years ago I worked with Beatrice Lillie on tour, playing the piano, and she had an unerring sense of what was funny. We had a matinee crowd in Palm Beach, and she had to make an entrance that had always gotten a laugh before, a piece of business with a fur coat. But when she did it that afternoon, there was absolute silence. She got up, took the fur coat with her, went back out the scenery door, came back in, and did the same bit again. Then she did it a third time, and by that time the audience was in the aisles. So it's like saying, "I believe that is funny whether you think so or not." You and I have somewhat different senses of humor. I love things that are dirty or risqué, and I encourage your vulgar streak whenever I possibly can.

EBB: Yes, you keep me vulgar. In *Over & Over*, our show based on Thornton Wilder's *The Skin of Our Teeth*, I wrote a line, "She's fucking the producer of the show." Joe Stein, who wrote the book, said, "I've never used the word 'fuck' in anything that

I've ever written." I was ready at that point to take it out and change it. But you said, "No, that's funny. Keep it. It's my favorite line." When we finally read the show for prospective producers, that line received a good response. I need the validation of people telling me whether or not a line is funny, and that has been an undercurrent through all my professional life. Hearing applause after one of our numbers is performed means the world to me. There is more of that in me than you, that need for validation. Oddly enough, I seldom approve totally of what I've written, but most of the time I do fully approve of what you have written.

KANDER: That's funny. I think of it the other way around.

EBB: Once many years ago I attended an afternoon of scenes that had been cut from various shows. I don't remember who put the afternoon together or how I even happened to be there, but they did scenes that had been taken out of shows like *Mister Roberts*. There were some incredibly funny scenes, and the lesson of the afternoon was that for the good of the whole show you often have to remove scenes. It may hurt you enormously to take them out. But they can be giant laughs that impede the project as a whole.

KANDER: Sometimes when people see one of our pieces that have been cut, they say, "That's really good. Why did you take that out?"

EBB: We had a number like that called "This Life" in *The Skin of Our Teeth* when we did it in Arlington a few years ago.

KANDER: If it weren't for Dorothy Loudon performing that piece, we would have probably cut it earlier. The character that Dorothy Loudon played was a character that we created for her.

EBB: Dorothy was a given in the casting, and she was wonderful. But the character didn't belong in the show. It wasn't Dorothy's fault. She was a name and a pal and we felt we had to write for her. So we wrote a number that did stop the show.

KANDER: She was very funny doing it, but it had nothing to do with the piece. When it's really clear like that, it's not a hard choice to make.

EBB: We knew that was the right choice. We were going to lose a showstopper, but we hoped the show itself would be better.

• • •

A somewhat scaled-down version of *Chicago* opened at the City Center Encores on May 2, 1996, then transferred to the Shubert Theater on November 14 that same year. The revival was one of the most lauded shows of recent years. The cast included Ann Reinking as Roxie, Bebe Neuwirth as Velma, and James Naughton as Billy Flynn. The production was directed by Walter Bobbie and choreographed by Ann Reinking "in the style of Bob Fosse."

• • •

KANDER: The *Chicago* revival started the night that we finished the dance auditions for *Steel Pier*.

EBB: We went to see the Encores' presentation at the City Center.

KANDER: We hadn't been to rehearsals. Johnny Mineo was in the company of *Chicago* and he had auditioned for *Steel Pier*. We saw him leaving the studio and asked him, "How's it going over there with *Chicago*?" He looked at us very strangely, and blinked, and said, "Oh, I think you're going to like it."

EBB: He didn't know how the audience would react.

KANDER: No, but he was happy and I've always remembered his reply because that was the understatement of the year.

EBB: We were both exhausted and neither one of us even

wanted to go see the show. On the way, we stopped off at a deli-catessen and had a sandwich, and then we literally trudged up to the City Center.

KANDER: But as we walked through the theater door, the atmosphere was all of a sudden electric. You could sense it almost before the show started.

EBB: What happened that night was astonishing.

KANDER: I don't think I have ever been through anything like it.

EBB: It was like we had invited everyone in the audience.

KANDER: They went nuts about vamps and entrances and even the announcement of a character.

EBB: "And now the ladies of the Cook County Jail"— "Whoa!"

KANDER: "Whoa!"

EBB: It was unbelievable, and I was not surprised that all of the producers in the audience were after it at the end. If I was a producer, I would have been after it too. I doubt that City Center ever had that kind of a reaction to a musical before. I had never seen anything like that. It was like hysteria.

KANDER: It was like a rock concert.

EBB: We didn't sit together, and you came over to me during the intermission. I remember your mouth was wide open, and I was just sitting there totally stunned. I couldn't even move. You said, "What do you think?" I said, "Jeeesus, this is amazing!" You can't account for a success like that. Don't even try.

KANDER: I remember telling you, "What is amazing is that it's the same orchestrations, the same dialogue snipped a bit, the same choreographic style as the original production."

EBB: What was different was the presentation. It was stripped down.

KANDER: The original production wasn't lavish.

EBB: But there was scenery, whereas there was no scenery in

this revival, so the songs were sort of in your face. Most of the performers came down center stage and sang to you.

KANDER: I think you're right not to try to figure it out, because it was still the same funny, nasty piece that it had been. Reviews for the original production were very mixed and critics who hadn't liked it suddenly liked the revival. Then they would try to explain why they had changed their minds.

EBB: I think that the audience caught up with the show, and history has been a great friend to us. We are living in a time of sensational murders and people either getting away or not getting away with them depending on what you believe. We have been helped enormously by the O. J. Simpson case, presidential adultery, and similar stories that suddenly had our sort of jaundiced worldview in the headlines.

KANDER: I guess it proves, much to our delight, that corruption never goes out of fashion. But I think, if anything, the success of *Chicago* is a little bit like the history of *Pal Joey*, which was originally considered just too mean in spirit. Then it was revived and was a big hit.

EBB: What we hear most often about *Chicago* is that it was ahead of its time.

KANDER: I don't really know what that means.

EBB: I don't know either, but for God's sake, what does anything mean! I'm just grateful. That opening at City Center was a night I will never forget.

KANDER: That was probably the most unique night in our entire careers. We went into the theater with no expectations except *Won't it be nice to see* Chicago *again*.

EBB: We were tired that night, but by the end of the performance I had so much energy that I was bounding up the staircase to see the performers.

KANDER: And you don't bound.

EBB: No, I certainly don't bound. Again, it says how fortunate we are. Individual shows get revived all the time but when you have two sensational productions of two shows at the same time as we do with *Chicago* and *Cabaret*, it really is something extraordinary. Last night I watched *Chicago* again, and this is its fifth year in revival. I sat there remembering the original cast— Gwen Verdon, Chita Rivera, and Jerry Orbach. I thought, *My God, this show is still running, and some of it is still funny, and the score is still decent. How lucky can you get?* It could have been anybody's show, given that cast and Bob Fosse's staging. Years later it was the perfect revival at the perfect time, but that's just luck.

And I remembered Bobby. Mean, brilliant, friend, companion. Helpful, lovable Bobby. After all these years, how I miss him. How grateful I was to him, how much he taught me and in a funny way how much I was able to teach him. Maybe even about love and forbearance. It's hard to know now. All I knew then was that he was an indelible part of my life and I would never forget him. And despite everything, there I was, looking at our brainchild. Oh, God, it was complicated, but I was grateful to him. Above all, I was grateful.

SIX

The Act and Woman of the Year

*T*he *Act* was a flashy, Las Vegas–style vehicle for Liza Minnelli, but the production, directed by Martin Scorsese, was beset during its pre-Broadway tryouts with rewrites, conflicts, and firings. Out of his element in musical theater, Scorsese retained his credit but was replaced by Gower Champion, who pulled the show together in time to win an enthusiastic reception for its star. The first Broadway show with a top ticket price of twenty-five dollars, *The Act* opened at the Majestic Theater to mostly favorable reviews October 29, 1977, and ran for 233 performances.

• ○ •

EBB: We first met Martin Scorsese when he worked with Liza on the movie *New York, New York*. For the title song, his request was for us to write a number that would score better than "And the World Goes 'Round," which we also wrote for that movie.

KANDER: It had to be that title, "New York, New York."

EBB: As a matter of fact, that's not the title. The title of that song is actually "The Theme from *New York, New York*."

KANDER: That's right. There was the threat of a lawsuit.

EBB: We received a letter from Betty Comden, Adolph Green, and Leonard Bernstein about the title. While you cannot copyright a title, as we came to understand it, there's an implied right, which means that if the first song was famous, the second song would seem to be trading on that fame if you used the same title. Their posture was that their "New York, New York" from *On the Town* was that famous, and we deferred to them.

KANDER: We had no choice but to write it anyway. For Bernstein's seventy-fifth birthday, I think, John Corigliano wrote a piece in which the two songs chase each other. Steve Sondheim sent me a recording of it. It's a funny piece of writing, a big orchestral piece, and, as I recall, the Boston Symphony performed it. In any case, we delivered five songs for the movie, including our first version of the title song. We played them for Liza and Scorsese.

EBB: And for Robert De Niro. I remember that he was sitting on a couch when we were at the piano in the office.

KANDER: Marty and Liza liked all of them. After the two of them told us how pleased they were, we started to leave until we saw this gesture from the couch—from De Niro. Marty went over to him and the two of them had a very animated, hand-waving kind of conversation. Then Scorsese came back to us and was very diplomatic with what he had to say at that point.

EBB: In Oscar Levant's book *A Smattering of Ignorance*, there is a chapter in which he suggests that when the boss calls you in and starts to compliment you, you know you are about to be fired. Marty started to go on effusively about how he much loved "And the World Goes 'Round," one of the five songs we had played for them. Then came the firing. He said, "But you know, your 'New York, New York' is not as strong as that number. So we wonder if you would take another pass at it."

KANDER: One of the reasons that De Niro was so concerned about the number was that "New York, New York" in the movie was a song that his character was writing. At that point, we were very thin-skinned about his request for a rewrite, like how could an actor be telling us how to write the song. Of course, we agreed that we would take another pass at it, but we weren't smiling. I don't remember what room we wrote it in, but the rewrite couldn't have taken us more than an hour. In a very short time, we wrote the current version of "New York, New York," which of course became a hit and was a hundred times better than what we had originally written.

EBB: We wound up being grateful for his request after we had first taken umbrage. What is umbrage anyway?

KANDER: If it wasn't for De Niro, we would never have written "New York, New York."

EBB: That's right. He ought to be coauthor.

KANDER: The fact is that he was right. The other song really was weak, so weak that neither of us can even remember it.

EBB: The first version was about going around in a hansom in the park.

KANDER: It was trite and familiar.

EBB: Like springtime is lovely with the birds in Central Park.

KANDER: But I think one of the strengths of "New York, New York," the final song, derived from the fact that we were miffed when we were writing it.

EBB: The vamp makes that song. That song is famous for the vamp, the interior melody that leads into it.

KANDER: The vamp came from the lyric. I was playing the piano, and dum dum da de dum came from "Start spreading the news . . ." That's the vamp.

EBB: Apparently, I wrote the lyric first, or at least the opening, umbrage and all. What is umbrage anyway?

KANDER: What still makes me smile is knowing that when we wrote it our attitude was "We'll show that actor!" But had De Niro not dissented we would never have written the biggest single hit we ever had in our lives.

EBB: It would not have gone through if it wasn't for De Niro, though the song was not a hit in the movie. It didn't break out until a few years later, when Sinatra sang it.

KANDER: As you know, the worst thing that you can say to me is "Give me a terrific vamp." I'll freeze if you say that. The vamp at the front of "New York, New York" is simply part of the tune. There are also vamps in *Cabaret* and other shows of ours. But I don't sit down and say, "Now I'm going to write a vamp." If I try that, I become very tense. I also become uncomfortable if we try to work outside our own style. We were asked to do a song in *The Act*, and the choreographer, Ron Lewis, wanted it to be a rock song. I resisted writing that number for a long time, and then I tried it. I was miserable doing it, and I think it even went into the show. It was dreadful.

EBB: "Hot Enough for You?"

KANDER: I wrote the song, and it's too bad, because it's like me trying to speak Romanian, trying to improvise in a language I don't speak.

EBB: That's funny. I speak fluent Romanian, but "Hot Enough for You" really was uninspired, though I remember when we played it for Marty Scorsese he said that he really liked it.

KANDER: I think I'm old enough now not to let myself do that anymore. Many people make that kind of stylistic transition and do it wonderfully. It's just not what I do. While we are usually attracted to the same material, I think you were more interested in *The Act* than I was. Is that true?

EBB: *The Act* was strange in many ways. Actually, Marvin Hamlisch came to us and his idea was that I write the first act with you and the second act I was to write with him. That was the arrangement he proposed, wasn't it?

KANDER: Originally, Marvin wanted you to write it with him, and then he suggested as a compromise that we somehow split the score.

EBB: That wasn't what I wanted to do, and we turned him down.

KANDER: That was really an act of loyalty on your part. My feeling about the material was that I wasn't sufficiently interested in the predicament of those characters.

EBB: I was more interested than you. I liked the idea of doing a club act on Broadway with a narrative stemming from the club act. *The Act* is about an actress who has had a screen career but suddenly discovers there is no work for her. She says to herself that she is going to get back in the arena and decides to go to Vegas to do a nightclub act. *The Act* was really about reclaiming success. You know, like the old Shirley MacLaine saga. The conceit was that the show would be put together like a nightclub revue, for which the score wasn't all written by one person. Although I like Marvin very much, I wouldn't do it without you, and the idea of splitting the score was not anything either of us wanted to do.

KANDER: We both like Marvin as a friend.

EBB: As I recall, he bowed out because the project wasn't going the way he envisioned. Then quite a few other people came to bear. Stanley Donen was in on it for a while, and George Furth was in on it from the beginning. I couldn't even begin to tell you all of the rewrites for *The Act*. We made changes out of desperation to try to make the show work. We started the show with one idea, which was that none of the songs would relate to the plot. It was to be a club act going on at the time the heroine was reminiscing about her life. But the audience kept looking for a connection. What was the connection between the club act and the rest of the scenes? That required an entirely different approach. That's when you know you are in deep trouble, when you have to change ideas midstream because you really haven't been sure of what the concept is. We've had shows that won strong critical approbation—*The Act* was one, at least with the New York critics—that I thought were actually rather sloppy efforts on our part. *The Act* later squeaked by mainly because of Liza's phenomenal energy. I thought there were some decent numbers in it, but not until we finally arrived in New York.

KANDER: With that piece, we were at a total loss. Marty Scorsese never should have done that show. We had some kitchen discussions about that before we went out to California. It was very strange that Liza did that show with him.

EBB: She was smitten with him.

KANDER: I think she always believed that somehow we could get her out of any jam, and, in fact, that was often the case, certainly, for you, Freddy. *The Act* was the wrong situation for Scorsese. I don't believe he had ever walked on a stage before and he and Liza were into this nutsy relationship, about which I knew very little. I didn't even know anything about cocaine at that time. They would come to rehearsal late all the time, very late. What was the one about the accident?

EBB: Oh, that was awful and really very hard on all of us. There was a day when we had a rehearsal at ten in the morning and the two of them weren't there. The entire cast was there. She didn't show up, and he didn't show up, and it got to be like twelve, one o'clock. When they finally came in, they said that they had been in a terrible accident on the freeway. The car they were in was totaled, and the cops took them in to some sort of holding station. Liza said, "Oh, they separated us because men and women can't go in there together," and then it all started sounding very, very strange. You took one look at her and you knew it was a lie. I wanted to say, "Why are you doing this?" That was a terrible day. I think Liza had a certain problem with reality, and maybe she still does. It seemed to me that she had a pretty active other life going on, a parallel life to what was going on in the theater.

> ### Liza Minnelli on alcohol and drug abuse:
>
> You have to remember at the point where I started to go through this, they didn't have all the information that they have now on this life-threatening disease. According to the AMA, alcoholism is obsessive-compulsive behavior. It's documented now, it's all in black and white. They didn't know those facts back then, so John and Fred saw something happening to me that they didn't understand. But they were there for me anyway. Only it wasn't me, it was circumstances and a disease. Nobody else understood, but they somehow kept faith, and I never let them down theatrically.

KANDER: There was never anything unpleasant about Marty.

EBB: I'm sure the rest of the cast thought the situation was unpleasant.

KANDER: But I mean he was not pulling the star thing. He was just in the wrong place. He would come to rehearsals and tape everything. Then he would go home and edit it.

EBB: He put it on a television.

KANDER: In a way, I understand what he was doing. It was like he was going to direct this piece within a technique that he understood.

EBB: Block it like a movie.

KANDER: But theater doesn't work that way, and Liza kept trying to make excuses for him. I don't know if you will agree with me or not, but I think there came a point when she knew the show was not working. She was never going to turn on him. She was never going to be the one to go to the producers and allow them to fire Marty. But I remember one of those late-night conversations with her where, without saying so, she was telling us to fix the situation.

EBB: She had to have been aware that the show wasn't working. The audience reaction was hideous. All she had to do was look out in the audience after intermission. Half of them were gone.

KANDER: Deep down inside, she wanted to be saved, but she did not want to be the one to have to be the bad guy, and nobody was brave enough to say anything to her.

EBB: I wondered what Marty thought about how the show went because he never came back like a Hal Prince might have done. In that same situation, Hal might have said, "Oh, my God, the show's not working," and wrung his hands. Scorsese never did that.

KANDER: But he wasn't there much of the time, Freddy.

EBB: He must have known. We were reviewed in all the papers while we were out of town. Marty had Jay Cocks from *Time* come to see *The Act*, and apparently Cocks told him the show wasn't working.

KANDER: There was one night after talking with Scorsese, I discovered he hadn't been there. We had three boys and there was a cover for the boys. One of the three, a guy named Michael Leeds, had dark hair and he had been out with back trouble. His cover, who was very blond, had been on all week. I was standing backstage with Marty when the cover, the blond kid, walked by. Marty asked me, "Who is that?" I said, "That's Michael Leeds's understudy. He's been on all week." Then, slow-witted as I am, I began to realize that Marty hadn't seen the show all week.

EBB: What was surprising was the type of questions Marty would ask. "What's a swing?" "What's a wagon?"* He would ask questions like that and I realized that he had never been anywhere near musical theater.

---

*A *swing* is a dancer who can fill in when necessary for other performers in a show. A *wagon* is the means by which a piece of scenery is moved on stage.

KANDER: This went on all the while we were in rehearsals and out of town. We first played Chicago, then San Francisco, then Los Angeles.

EBB: During all that time, the atmosphere was roiling.

KANDER: It was a very uncomfortable situation, though nobody was mean. Cy Feuer was one of the producers, and he would sit in the back of the theater every night taking copious notes. At one time, Cy had been a stage manager and he was knowledgeable, but he realized there was no point in giving his notes to Scorsese because Marty would never execute any of them. That was so frustrating, watching him with these big yellow sheets of paper. At the end of the night, Cy would look at his notes, then give a deep sigh and just tear them up.

EBB: The terrible thing was that we never failed to sell out. When we were due in San Francisco from Chicago, on one of the front pages of the newspaper was a picture of the lines around the block to buy tickets for *The Act*. That was scary for us, to know that we had all these audiences and no real show.

KANDER: I don't know what Cy said to Scorsese or how they got out of that commitment. That was done without us, thank goodness.

EBB: We were no braver than Liza was.

KANDER: No, because it wasn't as if we were going to be getting rid of someone we didn't like or someone who was unpleasant. There was never anything malevolent about Marty. We knew he was in over his head and that nothing would change as long as he was directing. The trouble was no one could confront Liza with the truth about the show's lack of direction.

EBB: We were in San Francisco when Michael Bennett was brought in as a possible replacement. Ron Field was there because he happened to be with Michael that night.

KANDER: Michael Bennett and Ron Field proceeded to give us no advice whatsoever, but at great length. Between the two of them, that was one of the most agonizing evenings in my life.

EBB: That was a terrible night, and they gave us strange advice. But they were asked by the producer to attend the show, at least Michael was, and we were summoned.

KANDER: We all sat there, a small audience, listening to them.

EBB: Liza and Cy Feuer were there too. We met in somebody's apartment, and both Michael and Ron held forth on what was wrong with the show. I remember one thing they said. When Liza first appears onstage, she should be in a large gray wig, and she should be an older woman making a comeback in a club, not the younger person that we portrayed. They wanted to have her be middle-aged. I didn't think much of any of their ideas.

KANDER: There was something that night that made my heart sink. We were hoping that they would come in and take over. But instead Michael Bennett gave us the most useless piece of advice about Scorsese. He said, "You've just got to help that poor baby." That sentence rang in my ears. I thought, *What can he be thinking?*

EBB: Oh, I could say more. I had the feeling they were stoned.

KANDER: Well, they were stoned a great deal of the time.

EBB: That also undercut their advice. Later, when we were in Los Angeles, one of the producers asked Gower Champion to see the show.

KANDER: It must have been Cy.

EBB: Gower came to a matinee, and then I took him home with me, and I must have had scabs on my knees from pleading with him to come in. "Please, Gower, just make it look professional." Liza was badly costumed. The lighting was awful. How humiliating it was to come in with a show that wasn't working for mechanical reasons.

KANDER: Gower saw at once what the problems were.

EBB: But he said, "I don't want to do it. I don't like the show. I think Liza is wonderful and I like the score. But I can't see this show working." I pleaded with him to come back to see the evening performance, and he did come back. After the show, he went into the dressing room with Liza and had a confab about what to do. Then he came out saying he would do it. What did he say, she was a "temptress"?

KANDER: I was going to have dinner with him, and I was waiting for her. Gower said, "I'm just going to go in and say a couple of things to Liza and then we'll all go out to dinner." This was right after the performance. So I waited, and I waited, and it was almost an hour later. I can't remember now whether we all went out or I went home, but I remember his reaction was: "She is a *temptress.*" That was his word.

EBB: God only knows what happened between them, but he agreed to do it, and he was an enormous help. The show at least began to look like a polished presentation, maybe of dog shit material, but the lights and costumes worked. The reviews had been awful in California, terrible in Chicago, hideous in San Francisco, but then there were good reviews in New York. It was almost a case of reverse snobbery.

KANDER: Granted that Liza was very seductive and that Gower enthralled her, but he was also somebody who was very definite in rehearsal. Even though the show was never wonderful, he made it immensely better and made her immensely better because she had somebody strong at the helm. He turned it into a show, and we were extremely grateful to him.

EBB: Oh, God, yes. Gower was like a savior.

KANDER: Gower saved us. He was totally different than he had been on *The Happy Time,* when he kept us out of rehearsals. When it came to *The Act,* he wanted us there all the time.

EBB: I think he needed us there because that was a show already scripted and formulated, whereas he was starting from scratch with *The Happy Time*.

KANDER: He did an interesting thing which for that show was perfect. He took the songs in the show and he made cards for each number. Then he arranged them on a table to see what the balance of the score was like, what followed what and what impact each would have with an audience. Before Gower came on, the numbers that she was singing in her act were non sequiturs and didn't relate to her story. Gower told us, "Fellas, you have to connect them." He was absolutely right, and he made the show make sense in a way that it had never made sense before.

EBB: Gower also went into the show after a while. He played the lead for a time after it opened in New York. I had forgotten that.

KANDER: He played the show for a couple of weeks. He was never a major actor, but he was all right.

EBB: Do you remember the S & M song we wrote for *The Act*?

KANDER: I thought that song was terrific.

EBB: It was in *The Act* for a time, though we didn't open with it. It was about a girl who liked to be smacked around. I love to write about offbeat subjects like that.

KANDER: The girl in that song was brought up like her mother to be a very good girl and always say, "Yes, sir. Please, sir. Thank you very much, sir." She marries and becomes very rich, which was her ascent into society.

EBB: But then she picks up guys who are going to hit her.

KANDER: She has her chauffeur drive her down to the docks to find guys who would beat her up.

EBB: [*singing*] "James, drive me to the docks again."

KANDER: [*singing*] "Down where the river flows? Hey, Mister. Are you calling me, honey?"

EBB: At the end it was "Yes, sir. Please, sir. Thank you very much, sir."

KANDER: As he beats her up. [*singing*] "Little girls who always watch their manners / Turn out to be ladies . . ."

EBB: We kidded each other about that for a long time. But we were supposed to write Liza's club act credibly, and we were looking for as much variety for her as we could find. Because the character she portrayed was a woman who had been a movie star and was now doing a club act to make a comeback, we made a decision that she should sing something highly dramatic and a little shocking to cast her out of her former image. She had always been the girl next door in the movies. So we asked ourselves what could she sing that was really very grown-up and shocking.

KANDER: You told me that Liza never liked that song.

EBB: No, she didn't. I don't think the audience liked that song either. That was why we finally cut it. I know that it was later done in a nightclub act by a Latin American woman, Aurelia.

KANDER: Right. She was Brazilian or Argentinian.

EBB: "Please, Sir" was her big number. She had a following and her audiences would ask her to sing that song all the time. Can you imagine? We've written a lot of made-to-order songs like that. Write an S & M song. Write about baseball. Write a Noel Coward song. Write a song about abortion. They were specific assignments.

KANDER: We've done that kind of thing a number of times. Remember "What's the Hurry, Larry?"

EBB: Oh yeah, that was about a girl—

KANDER: On her way to have an abortion. We wrote that song for a PBS television show about birth control.

EBB: And Larry was speeding. [*singing*] "Must you go so fast?" He apparently wanted to get there fast because he didn't want her to back out.

KANDER: That was your idea.

EBB: I love to write material like that.

KANDER: I remember Hal asked us to write a couple of

songs for *Diamonds*, which was a revue about baseball. We wrote a song about this organist, a woman who plays the organ at the baseball game. She studied for years to be this great organist, and now she's playing for baseball games.

EBB: We wrote that?

KANDER: I thought it was funny.

EBB: That was not a successful show, and in my memory our work was not all that good. I loved writing for the revival of *Hay Fever* [*December 12, 1985, Music Box Theater*]. We were asked to write a Noel Coward–type of song for Rosemary Harris to sing at a piano. The song worked fine, and everyone seemed pleased with it, which was pleasing to us.

KANDER: "No My Heart" was the title, and it really was a kind of Noel Coward song. Brian Murray directed that piece and I ran into him in the elevator the other day. Brian was singing it in the elevator as we were going down.

EBB: We wrote another made-to-order song for *The Mad Woman of Central Park West* [June 13, 1979, 22 Steps Theater]. Arthur Laurents directed that and he asked us for a number for Phyllis Newman.

KANDER: What was that song? It was kind of nice.

EBB: That was called "Cheerleader," and at the end she had a nervous breakdown. [*laughing*] But don't we all! At the end the poor lady was taking lithium. I actually don't remember seeing Phyllis perform it. I didn't see that show. Did you see it?

KANDER: I remember seeing her do it. I like Phyllis.

EBB: So do I. We just wrote the number and they seemed to like it. Then it was in the show, and that's all I know.

KANDER: One thing that all of those songs have in common, whether they work or not and whether anybody will ever sing them again, they really were all great fun to write.

● ● ●

With a book by Peter Stone and directed by Robert Moore, *Woman of the Year* was based on the 1941 Tracy/Hepburn movie. After opening at the Palace Theater on March 29, 1981, the show became a Tony-winning vehicle for its star, Lauren Bacall, and for Kander and Ebb. The songwriters crafted the score for performers who were not major singing talents and yet the show managed a Broadway run of almost two years, with Raquel Welch and later Debbie Reynolds following Bacall in the lead role. The original cast also included Harry Guardino, Roderick Cook, Rex Everhart, and Marilyn Cooper.

●　◦　●

KANDER: Peter Stone came to us with the idea for *Woman of the Year*, and Bacall was built into it from the beginning.

EBB: I think *Woman of the Year* was a mistake. We did that show because it was Lauren Bacall and it was a good title. But I didn't have any real conviction or passion about it. We won Tonys but mostly because there was nothing much up against us.

KANDER: That was another show where I don't think our work was so great. It's been a lesson to me that there are shows we have done which I think were really good but received no attention at all—I mean, major flops—and then suddenly we get a Tony Award for a show that is just professional.

EBB: We were up against a couple of shows that year that I had never even heard of. But it was still a pleasure to win it, and we loved Bacall.

KANDER: Oh, she was great with us.

EBB: I had a fantastic time with that lady. We had established early on a funny thing between us, when she called the house one day. I answered the phone and she said, "Hello." I said, "Hello, Jimmy." I was absolutely convinced that she was Jimmy Coco, with whom I had been playing poker regularly. "This is not

Jimmy," said the voice. I said, "Oh, come on, Jimmy, I have to be somewhere. Don't hold me up. What do you want?" She said, "I don't want anything." She would not let me off the hook, and I kept calling her Jimmy.

KANDER: She is Jimmy to this day.

EBB: Finally, she said, "This is Lauren Bacall," and the nickname stuck. She loved teasing me.

KANDER: She likes being Jimmy and we liked that it was something special between us. To this day, when she leaves a message on the service, she says, "Hello, this is Jimmy calling." I'm sure that we have the same reaction to her. There are a lot of social situations where I become self-conscious and unhappy and shy, but somehow if she's in the room I always feel better. It's funny to talk about her as a pal, but she is pal-like in our relationship with her. There are stories about how difficult she could be, but she was never that way with us.

EBB: Those stories come from people who don't really know her, like a hairdresser or a chauffeur. She could be a little rough on underlings.

KANDER: With her peers she was wonderfully gracious.

EBB: Yes, with other actors. She was very generous with Marilyn Cooper, who was stealing the show. At eleven o'clock, this little gnome came on and walked away with it.

KANDER: When we were working on the show out of town, if a number didn't work and had to be replaced, Bacall always took responsibility for it. Nobody else has ever done that with us. She would say, "That's really a terrific number, and I wish I had the voice to sing it."

EBB: We had a big showstopper with "The Grass Is Always Greener." The song came very late in the second act, and afterwards there was nothing in particular for Bacall to do. We had a meeting with the producers, Larry Kasha and David Landay, and Jimmy was there. They told us that after "The Grass Is Always

Greener" she had to have a big number like "New York, New York." I said, "Well, who's gonna sing it?" And Jimmy screamed with laughter. She thought it was hilarious that somebody would say a thing like that with her in the room. She said, "You know, he's right. I can't handle a song like that."

KANDER: We first met Tommy Tune when he came out of town to help us stage a number for *Woman of the Year*.

EBB: A number called "I Wrote the Book." I don't know why that was giving Tony Charmoli problems, but Tommy came and actually he staged it on me. I guess I walk like Bacall. I'm about as graceful as she is. It was less choreography than staging.

KANDER: Tony Charmoli was the choreographer, and how they got to the point where they called Tommy in I don't remember either. Tommy sort of comes in and out of our lives. I think we had met before but never worked together.

EBB: Yes, we met Tommy before we did *Woman of the Year*.

KANDER: You remember the pitcher of water? Somebody came up with the idea that just before the end of the show—

EBB: Jimmy was to get drenched.

KANDER: The guy who was playing opposite her was to take a pitcher of water and throw it in her face.

EBB: Over her head really.

KANDER: Nobody wanted to tell her because we were all afraid. We were in Boston at the Sheraton Hotel, and all of us wanted to get her to try the scene, and nobody had the courage to ask her. But you did. You were the brave one.

EBB: I just figured, she's our pal and if she doesn't want to do it, that's her choice. But the scene would probably be funny, and the audience wants her to get soaked by that point in the show.

KANDER: Bacall's reaction was perfect. "Sure, I'll try it. I'll try anything. Do you really think it will get a laugh?"

EBB: It did, and it got a big hand too.

KANDER: It also gave her a curtain call because she came out with the bathrobe—

EBB: And towel.

KANDER: With quite a few people that we have worked with, when we know that something is built into the show, that person will try anything.

EBB: Gwen Verdon was another.

KANDER: And Lotte Lenya, who we've mentioned. If you know Lenya is going to be there and her voice is in the back of your head, it's not that you say to yourself, "How am I going to tailor it for her?" It's just that you listen to the sound of that voice and it guides you. There was some of that with Bacall. We wrote songs that were so well suited for her that when other people sing them they are not quite the same. The show has been done a number of times, fortunately, but nobody really made it work like Bacall did, in large part because we had her in mind as we wrote.

EBB: I think that's true. I remember Raquel Welch and Debbie Reynolds in the role.

KANDER: With each of those ladies we had to make adjustments to make it work.

EBB: Raquel was breathtakingly beautiful and wore wonderful costumes. She was the kind of woman who got a hand when she entered because of how stunning she looked. The body was perfect, and the audience would applaud just for her walking out there. She didn't play the part as well as Jimmy—nobody could—but she brought something else to it. The audience thoroughly enjoyed her.

KANDER: Raquel knew where to take the water. When they were staging the scene, she said, "No, no, lower!"

EBB: She wanted a wet T-shirt.

KANDER: But she knew exactly what she was doing.

EBB: No one was ever surer of her sexuality than Raquel Welch. And good for her, why not?

KANDER: That was certainly the climax of the show. As the water descended and the outline of her breasts showed through, there was a gasp from the audience.

EBB: She worked very hard, and she delivered. I'd work with Raquel again in a minute. Debbie was fine also. However, Debbie had a propensity to ad-lib. When she thought a scene was not going entirely right, she managed to sneak in something about her husband or about Eddie Fisher. Out of her training, the Vegas stuff, came a sensibility that says you are allowed the freedom to do that on the stage. Steve and Eydie did the same thing in *Golden Rainbow*. I don't think they ever played the same show twice, because they would ad-lib whenever they thought they could get the audience to laugh along with them. Debbie had the same mentality. Bacall would not do that, and I don't think Raquel would have done it.

KANDER: Raquel just didn't understand where the jokes were.

EBB: But Debbie was sweet in the part, except for her ad-libbing. I remember there was one scene in a bar where she got started on something, and she went on about marriage and how you keep getting married until you get it right. The audience encouraged her, and she went on and on until it looked like a comedy monologue.

KANDER: I never saw that.

EBB: I was there, and it had nothing to do with the piece. But the audience loved it. Audiences love mistakes. They love any contact that assumes some special knowledge shared between the performer and themselves, which I think gives them a sense of power. But my woman of the year will always be Bacall, the glorious Jimmy now and forever.

SEVEN

The Rink and
Kiss of the Spider Woman

*T*he Rink reunited Chita Rivera and Liza Minnelli, but the stellar combination failed to ignite the musical when it opened at the Martin Beck Theater on February 9, 1984. Despite the show's unfavorable reception, Kander describes *The Rink* as "the most complete realization of our intentions on any production we have done." It also provided Rivera with her first Tony Award for her portrayal of Anna, the mother who owns the roller rink. Minnelli played the role of Angel, an ugly-duckling flower child who returns home after seven years only to discover the beloved roller rink of her childhood is now a derelict ruin awaiting demolition. Angel's conflict with her mother was illuminated by numbers like "Don't 'Ah, Ma' Me," "Chief Cook and Bottle Washer," and "All the Children in a Row." Directed by A. J. Antoon, *The Rink* lasted 204 performances and provided one of the most poignant Kander and Ebb moments with the song "Colored Lights."

● ● ●

KANDER: I loved doing *The Rink*.

EBB: I loved *The Rink*, too, though I've always been more susceptible than you are to bad reviews. I can be talked out of my pride in a show by bad reviews.

KANDER: That show was a very emotional, fulfilling experience. Whatever little ups and downs we had, it was a piece I was especially proud of. I thought it was directed and cast wonderfully. But we really got slammed.

EBB: It also looked fabulous on the stage.

KANDER: I went back all the time.

EBB: So did I. Initially, Liza wasn't supposed to be in it. Chita Rivera was already cast, and Liza called me in California and said, "Can I be in *The Rink*? I'll do anything. I'll take second billing. I'll bow next-to-the-last bow. I just want to be in it. I want to be with you guys and Chita."

KANDER: She called me too, separately. As I remember, she was in England when she made the call. I was telling her the same thing that I'm sure you told her. "It's really a second lead. You would be playing this schlumpy girl." But one of the things she said was, "I want to do the show because there's not one sequin in it." I thought that was a really understandable and bright thing to say.

EBB: If you were to ask me now, I would say that was an error.

KANDER: It turned out to be an error because the audience didn't want to see her without the sequins.

EBB: They were disappointed in the lack of sequins, though I thought she played the role beautifully. But we had made certain writing errors, and they were magnified because it was Liza. For instance, we had the song "Colored Lights" opening the show primarily because it was Liza, and we thought she's out there as the big star attraction. Now we see that was exactly the wrong thing to do. Our fault. Not hers.

I was sitting on a sand dune in Santa Cruz
Or Monterey.
Well, anyway,
I could feel the trickle on my cheek of ocean spray,

A perfect day.
Well, anyway,
I remember that I turned to Sam and said . . .
Or was it Fred? . . .
Well, anyway,
I should be up and yet I'm down instead.
Something's missing, Sam;
Something's missing, Fred.
Something's missing here.

Where are my colored lights?
Beads and bleachers and colored lights?
Passing smiles, 'round and 'round
Thumping oom-pah-pah organ sound.

Noisy boys, long and lean.
Giggles of girls in the mezzanine.
Filtered through colored lights,
Gold and amber and green.

I was sailing out of Long Beach on a catamaran
Or fishing scow.
Well, anyhow,
I was leaning, chewing cashews off the starboard bow.
That sunset: Wow!
Well, anyhow,
I remember telling Joey, "God, you're sweet!"
Or was it Pete? . . .
Well, anyhow,
I wonder why I feel so incomplete.
Something's missing, Joe;
Something's missing, Pete.
Something's missing here . . .

Where are my colored lights?
Beads and bleachers and colored lights?
Passing smiles, 'round and 'round
Thumping oom-pah-pah organ sound.

Noisy boys, long and lean.
Giggles of girls in the mezzanine.
Filtered through colored lights,
Gold and amber and green.

And I tried to find the answer in the friends I made,
Or beds I'd share,
Well, anywhere.
But with other people's music ringing in my ear
I couldn't sing,
Well, anything.
And I thought if I could just be twelve again,
Or was it ten? . . .
Well, anyway,
It seems to me I knew the secret then.
It's so simple: twelve.
It's so simple: ten.
It was simple there.
Passing smiles, 'round and 'round
Thumping oom-pah-pah organ sound.

Noisy boys, long and lean.
Giggles of girls in the mezzanine.
Filtered through colored lights,
Red and orange and gold and amber and pink and yellow and green.

Leaving home years ago,
What was I looking for?

I don't know.
I can't recall well, anyway.

Soon I'll have my days and nights of
Wonderful, glimmering, beautiful, shimmering
Colored lights!

KANDER: That piece was very special—

EBB: But Liza with a backpack and long, stringy hair?

KANDER: She looked marvelous!

EBB: But she was fat. She had all that weight. The audience didn't like that.

KANDER: Actually, the audiences were very responsive. They were on their feet every night.

EBB: For Liza and Chita. But the critics didn't like it.

KANDER: I don't think the mistakes that we made were large enough to account for why the critics took after us.

EBB: I don't know that we ever wrote anything much better than "Don't 'Ah, Ma' Me" from *The Rink*.

KANDER: That was one of the best lyrics you ever wrote. It was a confrontation between the mother and daughter early in the show, and it was furious:

Anna:
If the earth had opened up,
If it swallowed me inside,
Would my darling baby girl
Even realize I'd died?
You were sitting on a hill
With some yippie on your lap
Talking love and life and art
And that transcendental crap
With the dope I'm sure you smoke

And a healthy dose of coke
Up your nose.

Angel:
Ah, Ma.

Anna:
Up your nose.

Angel:
Ah, Ma.

Anna:
And for all you ever knew
I was hustling for the rent
'Cause you only called collect
Maybe every other Lent.
While I'm bleeding on the street
From some maniac's attack
You're in some Ramada Inn
Seeking wisdom on your back
Making kibble of your brain,
An emancipated pain
In the ass.

Angel:
Ah, Ma.

Anna:
In the ass.

Angel:
Ah, Ma.

Anna:
And don't Ah, Ma me.
You said you had to find yourself
So find yourself some other place
And don't Ah, Ma me.
I don't need you around
To help me complicate my life.

And if you really gave a damn
You'd have never stayed away.
When you break a mother's heart,
Does it make a guru's day?
But you're nearly thirty now
And you're panicked and upset
So you walk back in the door
And expect me to forget.
Welcome home, my little pig.
Boy, you really got a big
Set of balls.

Angel:
Ah, Ma.

Anna:
Some balls.

Angel:
Ah, Ma.

Anna:
And don't Ah, Ma me.
You said you had to find yourself
So find yourself some other place

And don't Ah, Ma me.
I don't need you around
To help me complicate my life, *capisce?*
Don't Ah, Ma me.
The sign on the apartment
Doesn't say Salvation Army, does it?
Don't Ah, Ma me.
I've heard it all your life
And I don't need to hear it now.

Angel:
Ah, Ma.

Anna: [*spoken*] Jesus!

Angel:
It's like it was before,
I just walk through the door
And right away you start to fight and curse.

Anna: [*spoken*] That's bullshit!

Angel:
Ma, I hoped there'd be some tears
And after all these years
You might have mellowed some
But Jesus, was I dumb.

Anna:
So you thought I might be calm,
Maybe jolly you along
But believe me I'm not calm
And believe me you were wrong.
Should the sound of your hello

Be like music to my ears
When I haven't seen your face
In, what is it, seven years?
Now you walk back in my life,
Should I really bless my luck?
That's an outfit you could wear
On a sanitation truck.
Have a daughter, I was told,
They're a blessing when you're old.
Ah, stroongatz.

Angel:
Ah, Ma.

Anna:
Stroongatz.

Angel:
Ah, Ma.

Anna:
Enough.

Angel:
Ah, Ma.

Anna:
That's it.

Angel:
Ah, Ma.

Anna:
Shut up.

Angel:
Ah, Ma.

Anna:
I quit.

Angel:
Ah, Ma.

Anna:
Now I got a good thing going
And I don't need you to hex it.
Did you notice where you enter
You can also make an exit?
So go out and find a husband,
Join a convent,
Be a whore
But I am sick and tired of your
Ah, Ma.

Angel:
Ah, Ma.

Anna:
Shush!

EBB: It was such a pleasure to write and I thought it was at least acceptable writing, but that song was never even mentioned in reviews. The music was so appropriate, and it was also so smart and so funny. [*laughing*] And unnoticed, and that hurts a person. It was up front, right at the start of the show. But nothing happened. We didn't score critically, though I think the audience might have enjoyed it. I was proud of our work, and it was so well performed. We had showstopping numbers. The number

"The Rink" did exceptionally well. "After All These Years" also did well for the guys who were the demolition crew. Jason Alexander was head of the crew, and we had Scott Ellis, another one who went on to do first-rate work in the theater.

KANDER: That was the first time we worked with Scott.

EBB: And Rob Marshall, who has now directed the movie of *Chicago*. Look what happened to him.

KANDER: We had worked with Robbie before. We first met him when he was in the chorus on *Zorba*, in the revival with Anthony Quinn. That was Rob's first job in New York. Later he was an understudy in *The Rink* and the dance captain. He became a part of that group of collaborators we worked with often.

EBB: I hope it's not sour grapes, but even today I really cannot understand why that show was attacked the way it was. Looking for reasons to make some sense of it, you come up with maybe it was Liza being too high-powered a personality for that role, or maybe we threw too much at them for what was essentially a slender story.

KANDER: I don't think any of those explanations amount to a hill of beans.

EBB: Because we've never come up with one. Maybe we should just take umbrage. *The Rink* seemed like it would be hard to go wrong with Terrence and Chita and Liza.

KANDER: I thought that Terrence McNally's book was terrific in drawing the relationship between the two women and the whole device of the six guys who played the other parts, all wonderfully talented men.

EBB: I wouldn't have given up the richness of that experience for anything. It's just too bad the actors didn't get more of a run out of it. I used to watch *The Rink* from the wings, and I never do that. There was such a feeling of camaraderie. There were seven of us, and we all huddled together and watched the numbers from the wings.

KANDER: The show ran most of the year.

EBB: Because we had those two ladies in it.

KANDER: People always get up at award shows and make speeches saying this show or that was such a loving experience. Usually they've forgotten or they're exaggerating. But this was the real thing, an extraordinary experience for all the people involved. I remember Jason Alexander backstage after the reviews came out, crying and saying, "They killed our baby!"

EBB: It was exactly that kind of feeling.

KANDER: The only thing that makes any sense to me is that at the time the show opened, we were still too close to the period of the sixties and seventies. Frank Rich particularly took great offense at how we were dealing with that generation.

EBB: He wrote something rather snotty. We had a song in it called—

KANDER: "All the Children in a Row."

EBB: In the middle of that song, we dramatized Liza's character and her boyfriend—

KANDER: Who was a hippie.

EBB: The boy said to her at one point—

KANDER AND EBB: "Where's Cambodia?"

EBB: It was intended to be gentle and funny.

KANDER: Oh, I thought it was touching and Scott Ellis delivered the line perfectly.

EBB: As in *Flora*, the characters in *The Rink* were caught up in a political cause about which they didn't know a hell of a lot. That's all I meant by that line.

KANDER: He was such an innocent.

EBB: He was a simple boy, and Cambodia seemed an exotic place. But Frank Rich went off on it scathingly. I think Frank Rich is a wonderful writer and most likely a very astute and bright guy. I was kind of annoyed that he didn't understand the real intent of that line "Where's Cambodia!" Then he went off on Terrence McNally and the whole show.

KANDER: I must have told you, after the reviews came out, Terrence went back to see Liza, who was crying because Frank Rich barely mentioned her in his review. She said, "He dismissed me in two sentences." And Terrence said, "You're lucky. He dismissed me in two very long paragraphs." He really savaged Terrence.

EBB: There was one line about Liza at the end, "Also appearing was Liza Minnelli." It was unbelievable. We had been delivering to the audiences, and the previews all went well. There was an effect at the end that is still one of the most beautiful moments that I ever saw in our shows, where all the scenery disappeared.

KANDER: They ended up transported out to the boardwalk.

EBB: And technically, the show worked. Everything was fine until we opened.

KANDER: Nobody can explain it, the experience when everything goes terrifically in previews, and you don't allow yourself to be deluded too much, but you think the audience is really loving it. Then opening night comes and the next thing you know you're dust.

EBB: That was one show that had enthusiastic audiences until we opened. *Cabaret*, on the other hand, had really dull, disbelieving, negative audiences.

KANDER: Until they were told.

EBB: After they were told it was a big hit, they were pushing each other out of the way to get into the theater. So it works both ways.

KANDER: With *70, Girls, 70*, during the weeks of previews the audiences were really hysterical with laughter. But once the bad reviews came out, we couldn't get anybody to laugh at the same jokes, the same performances.

EBB: The intimidation factor is enormous. Before *The Rink* closed, Liza was in bad shape and there was an intervention to get her into treatment.

KANDER: Intervention. Sounds like a musical, doesn't it?

EBB: She had missed a lot of performances during the run.

KANDER: Liza had really counted on that show to change her career, to allow her to be the actress that in fact she was and is. When that didn't happen, when the bad reviews came in, then bad stuff started happening with her. I think that hurt her tremendously. I don't know what other troubles were going on inside of her before that, but I know that she started having real problems after those reviews came out. I'm sure that reaction contributed to her addictions. I thought of her during those troubled times as like the Marilyn Monroe character in Arthur Miller's *After the Fall*, when she asks for pills and her husband tells her basically, "I won't be the one to give you death."

EBB: After *The Rink*, all Liza could do was go home and sew a sequin on her backpack.

KANDER: *The Rink* was a role where she didn't have to play Liza, and neither the public nor the critics wanted that. That had a tremendous effect on her, and she has never since, with all of her ups and downs, ventured too far from the image of Liza. Her success in London and New York this year [2002] is wonderful, but in a sense it's all about how marvelous it is that we've got the old Liza back. That's what they wanted.

EBB: That's what everybody wanted. It's funny because now I would have no interest in delivering that with her the way I did once. That whole arena of concerts doesn't interest me as much. If I were to do it, I would want to do an evening where she sits on a stool and just sings Charles Aznavour and Edith Piaf. But she can only get away with so much of that material in her concerts. She still has to go to "New York, New York" and "Cabaret" and the numbers the audience expects. It's a pity because she has done wonderful work as an actress, like *The Sterile Cuckoo*. I think she should be doing projects like *Come Back, Little Sheba*. Ah, hell, sometimes the critics confuse me and really hurt, and then all you can do is take cover, and, oh yes, take umbrage.

KANDER: I think Liza's a wonderful actress for a number of

Liza on "Liza's Back":

Look at "Liza's Back," the song they wrote for my recent tour. Fred said, "You come out and you say the truth. Don't hide behind anything. You have nothing to hide behind. You know what I mean. There's nothing wrong with what happened to you. It happened to you. So you talk about it before they do." I said, "Before they do?" He said, "It doesn't matter. You talk about it!" I said, "Yes, Freddy, you're right." The song was so funny, hilarious, and the people appreciated it because out of my mouth comes the truth. I think Fred's lyrics are ingenious:

I took my bottles of pills
And I flushed them away,
And I emptied the booze,
And I went to A.A.
Hey, London, Liza's back.
London, Liza's back
And that's okay.

And I went to a class
To get ready to dance,
And I dieted hard
'Til they took in my pants.
Hey, London, Liza's back.
London, Liza's back
And it's okay . . .

---

reasons, not the least of which is that she invents so much and makes it sound real. Terrence said once, "Liza can turn emotionally on a dime onstage." I don't know if she will ever be allowed to be the superb actress that she really is. Hopefully, she will later on. But she shouldn't at this point in her career allow herself to be a media freak. Liza should be a serious artist because she is one. I think it's unfortunate because there is a real actress missing that never had the chance to blossom. It wasn't her fault with *The Rink*.

EBB: She couldn't help being deeply disappointed by *The Rink*. All of us were. I remember nights when I had to take her to the emergency room of a hospital, once because she said someone stepped on her foot. She played the show in a cast for a while. That was all very weird.

KANDER: Chita could always tell at the beginning of the show whether she was okay or not. I never saw Liza fall apart onstage.

EBB: It was hard on Chita.

KANDER: Particularly because she is so disciplined.

EBB: Chita didn't like playing it with an understudy, and I didn't blame her. Everything in the show was put on both of them very carefully. A. J. Antoon had turned in a brilliant job directing.

KANDER: I thought his staging was gorgeous.

EBB: It was scholarly, the way he dissected that script and gave motivations to the actors. I wouldn't have changed a word, and I liked our contributions except for a couple of glaring exceptions. And you couldn't look up there and say, "Oh, God, I wish we'd cast it better."

KANDER: There was terrific bonding in that little company.

EBB: It was a pleasure to go backstage because everybody loved everybody.

KANDER: That's what I meant with what I said about Jason in tears. It was like they had taken this thing that we all loved and protected, and they killed it.

EBB: He was standing behind me one night during a preview performance. We were watching Chita and Liza doing a scene, and we looked out into the audience together. There were a lot of happy faces out there, and we were thrilled. He said, "God, we're gonna open soon." Then he squeezed my shoulder and said, "How could they not like this?"

KANDER: *Steel Pier* was also a show the critics attacked. But that was another one of those experiences like *The Rink*, during which it was a love fest.

EBB: [*laughing*] It shows you that we shouldn't do those.

• • •

With a libretto from Terrence McNally (based on Manuel Puig's novel), *Kiss of the Spider Woman* reunited Kander and Ebb with Harold Prince. Once again the team took on material that appeared to defy the musical form, but *Kiss of the Spider Woman* managed to counterpose totalitarian repression with camp in its male leads: a macho political prisoner (Valentin) and a gay window dresser (Molina) who is obsessed with movies. This controversial and startlingly artistic show developed from a 1990 workshop at State University of New York, Purchase. The show traveled to Toronto and London in 1992, then opened in New York the following year and played for 906 performances. *Kiss of the Spider Woman* earned seven Tonys, including Best Score for Kander and Ebb and Best Actress for Chita Rivera. The journey from workshop to Broadway exemplifies the perilous commercial realities of today's musical theater, with the show's corporate producer, Live Entertainment, declaring bankruptcy in 1998.

• • •

KANDER: On *Kiss of the Spider Woman*, Freddy, you came up with the idea. You said to me, "Kiss of the Spider Woman," and I said, "Yes!" immediately. The next person we spoke to was Hal Prince. We said the title, and Hal said, "Yes!" immediately. Everybody after that thought it was the worst idea they had ever heard, except for Terrence McNally. When we suggested that he do the book, we said the title to him and he also knew immediately what it was. No one else could imagine why anyone would want to tackle such a grim story. A musical about torture, homosexuality, and death?

EBB: There was no question this was going to be difficult material. It's hard for people to latch onto your vision and share your enthusiasm when the subject matter is difficult. I had read the book and seen the movie. I was more impressed with the book because I wasn't all that convinced by the Academy Award performance of William Hurt.

KANDER: It was the book that was the turn-on.

EBB: The book was much more involving to me, and it was because of the book that I approached you.

KANDER: It's easier to work from a book when you can really go inside the mind of the character. Immediately we saw musical, theatrical, possibilities in it to write and entertain us. It was perfectly obvious to the three of us that not only do you have the exotic locale of a South American prison, but you're spending half the evening inside of somebody else's fantasy, and if that isn't a clear message to do something musical, I don't know what would be. What seems unlikely musical material to many people often seems like very likely material to us. When you initially suggested *Kiss of the Spider Woman*, the first thing that came to mind was that this is a man who lives in his imagination, a man who's summoning up movies—how much more musical can you get than that? I think these pieces that are kind of bold—and particularly if they are exotic on top of it—are much easier to write than a little story about boy meets girl in New York. I don't know how to do that.

EBB: With *Kiss of the Spider Woman*, we had another advantage in that the novel's author, Manuel Puig, worked with us for some time before we started. Just absorbing him—his personality and insights—gave us a lot of clues into how to write "The Window Dresser's Song" and others like that. Manuel Puig himself was so flamboyant.

KANDER: When he talked about doing a tango, all of a sudden—

EBB: He would get up and do a tango.

KANDER: That's my first visual memory of him.

EBB: Dancing in Hal's office. Or he would do a samba. As writers, we tried to absorb his energy and joy and love in our work. We inherited that, or you could say we inhaled that.

KANDER: Hal arranged that collaboration. Puig was originally going to write the libretto for the show, but that didn't work out, really, although he stayed with it. English was a second language, which put him at some disadvantage writing a script. We never used Manuel's libretto, but he came to Purchase with us, and he was our conscience. He saw the show with the script that Terrence McNally wrote, and as I recall, Manuel was very supportive of the direction we were going and his comments were always very pertinent.

Hal Prince on Manuel Puig:

Puig was flamboyant and innocent, and his personality reflected everything that's in his material. The only problem was he lived part of the time in Buenos Aires and the rest in Rio and Cuernavaca. The absence of propinquity made it impossible for him to write the book. You need to be really there for each other while you're creating a musical.

KANDER: But that same year we were in Purchase, Manuel suffered this terrible, ridiculous death. It was a freak thing that should not have happened.

EBB: He apparently had a heart attack after an operation. I'll never forget having met him, as fantastic a human being as you would ever want to meet.

KANDER: He was really out of a Puig novel.

EBB: Yes, like he invented himself. When you put that personality on the stage in the hands of a brilliant actor like Brent Carver, you look good as a songwriter because it seems like you know more than you do.

KANDER: If you put Puig in that cell and call him Molina, that's what the story would be.

EBB: That's what I think too. *Kiss of the Spider Woman* had quite a long history. As a workshop at SUNY Purchase, it was a disaster.

KANDER: The idea of the "New Musicals" program at Purchase was to do a Broadway-size musical in a Broadway-size house. It was very luxurious for us to do a full production and to be able to look at it as if it were a workshop, rather than doing a tiny production. That was a great idea.

EBB: It was shot down.

KANDER: But it's still a great idea.

EBB: Hal is one of the great pioneers of musical theater and he is constantly looking for ways to promote what we do. You know, he didn't leave us for Hollywood and we didn't leave *him* for Hollywood. I think there is something admirable about people who stay in the theater without any particular aspirations beyond that.

KANDER: I think that's true. With *Kiss of the Spider Woman*, we were all in a state of outrage because the *Times* did a really terrible thing that nothing anyone could possibly say could justify. They insisted on reviewing the show even after seventeen people went down to the *New York Times* offices to ask them not to do so. These were not just people connected with our show but to other shows that were coming in and were going to be part of the workshop process in Purchase. *The Secret Garden, My Favorite*

Year, and a new musical by Erica Jong were also being planned for Purchase. We all begged the *Times* not to review the show.

Harold Prince on the *Times* review of *Kiss of the Spider Woman*:

The *Times* should never have gone to Purchase. Over the years of my career, the media has come to think of theater as another news story. Now they wonder why we have so many events and so little real theater. That's what news reporting is about: events. There is no isolation anymore while you fix a show. You can't go to New Haven or Boston, find yourself in trouble, roll up your sleeves, rewrite, restage, recast if necessary, and FIX without reading in the New York press what trouble you're in on the road. It's mean-spirited and trivializing. And the theater has suffered.

EBB: For us, it was like David against Goliath, and the *Times* was Goliath. It was grossly unfair to have the show reviewed by such a prestigious, influential newspaper, and by Frank Rich, no less. Not only did we get a reviewer but a really tough guy who hadn't particularly been a fan of ours. The *Times* considered it a news story, and also since we were charging admission, they argued that they should review it. It was most unfortunate because Frank Rich did come, he did not like it, and he did print his review. Because of the show's lackluster performance, we had to kill the whole project temporarily. More and more the theater is in trouble because it's all about reviews like that. It's about obscene amounts of money and critics who say, "Please take risks," but the shows that take risks usually don't win audiences. So it's a kind of catch-22.

KANDER: The workshop at Purchase was quite unique because you could put on a production and change it every night if you wanted to. The audience knew that, and you could sit and get feedback. During that period, you could learn about your show, then close it down, rewrite it, and go for a Broadway production. If we had not had that experience, the show would not have become what it did, and I wish to God there was someplace that you could work like that today. We were lucky because we did have a chance to see where we had gone wildly astray and later got picked up. We had been trying to tell two different stories at once, and the audience didn't follow it.

EBB: We did practically everything wrong. We made error after error, not only with the libretto but with the score. We wrote a couple of songs that were humiliating. We had a tap dancer in it, and I remember him because one night he went out to do his big tap number and forgot to put on his tap shoes.

KANDER: Right, he actually went out onstage and discovered that he didn't have any tap shoes.

EBB: So we had not only a bad number but a guy who was unable to perform without his shoes.

KANDER: We wrote song after song for one moment in *Kiss of the Spider Woman*, and I don't know how we ever came up with the last one.

EBB: Which was—

KANDER: "Where You Are." When we're stuck like that, the collaboration helps, just patiently working it out between us and drawing ideas from the libretto:

When you feel you've gone to hell in a hand basket
And the world in which you dwell's no paradise.
I've some counsel I can give, you need but ask it.
I'm so very glad to share this good advice:

You've got to learn how not to be where you are.
The more you face reality, the more you scar.
So close your eyes and you'll become a movie star.
Why must you stay where you are?

You've got to learn how not to see what you've seen.
The slice of hell you call your life is harsh and mean.
So why not lie beside me on a movie screen.
Why must you see what you've seen?

And if you find that you land in jail,
A little fantasy will not fail.
It's just as simple as "ABC."
Come up here.
Play with me.
Play with me.

You've got to learn how not to do what you've done.
The pistol shot can't kill if you unload the gun,
So, build a palace where you're the Shah
And we'll embrace in that Shangri-La.
If you run away
Some matinee
From where you are.

KANDER: With writers like Peter Stone and Terrence Mc-
Nally particularly, they will write a scene knowing full well that
we are probably going to steal from what they have written, that
we will incorporate material in the score that comes directly from
the book. Terrence will go to great lengths, as a matter of fact,
sometimes writing a whole speech expecting us to musicalize it,
as was often the case in his book for *Kiss of the Spider Woman*.

EBB: Terrence was always amenable and encouraging whenever we pilfered moments from his book.

KANDER: Terrence is very musical. He can sense when he
reaches a point that is probably going to need music. It's not that
he writes lyrics. He just indicates to us that this is a moment that
is probably going to be expressed musically.

EBB: We try to write in the rhythm of the libretto where a particular scene can suggest what needs to be done rhythmically in a number. That was certainly the case with *Kiss of the Spider Woman*.

KANDER: Garth Drabinsky is the person who saved us on that show. He came to Purchase and saw it. I don't know what went on between Garth and Hal, but eventually Garth as producer thought that there could be life in it. Then we spent the better part of a year reworking it. Hal had given Garth the biggest success of his life, which was *Phantom of the Opera* in Toronto.

EBB: If it were not for Garth Drabinsky, *Spider Woman* would never have opened. There is no reason in the world that show would have come in even with our names on it. But Garth had this steadfast belief in the project and in Hal's ability to bring in a winner. Unlike many other people, Garth did put his money where his mouth was. He was the knight in shining armor and will always be a hero of mine. He took us on and gave us everything that we needed. If there was a song that had to go and we needed to replace it with another number, a process which can be expensive with the orchestration and rehearsal time, he didn't balk at anything. You sensed his love for the creative process and the creators. He took us to Toronto first, where we started to put it into shape and Chita came into it. Then we went to London, where I became quite fond of it.

Harold Prince on bringing *Spider Woman* to Broadway:

Never underestimate the incredible satisfaction of having a show so savagely received two years earlier, and then taking it and coming back to the same New York arena and having a triumphant reception. That's unique in my life and wonderful.

EBB: I remember our first performance of *Kiss of the Spider Woman* in New York. I ran backstage at the end and there was Hal Prince all by himself. We immediately hugged and kissed simply because we were so thrilled. Whether the show was going to be a success or not really didn't matter. It was just that we had finally made it as good as we knew how to make it. Hal said, "Fred, it doesn't get much better than this!"

EIGHT

And the World Goes 'Round and Steel Pier

With an Off-Off-Broadway revival of *Flora, the Red Menace*, Kander and Ebb began a series of collaborations with three up-and-coming musical theater talents: director Scott Ellis, librettist David "Tommy" Thompson, and choreographer Susan Stroman. *Flora*'s book was rewritten by Thompson, while Kander and Ebb wrote several new songs and reinstated songs that had been cut in the 1965 production. The revival opened at the Vineyard Theater on December 6, 1987, and ran for forty-six performances, with Veanne Cox and Peter Frechette in the roles originally played by Liza Minnelli and Bob Dishy.

● ○ ●

EBB: Scott Ellis, David Thompson, and Susan Stroman brought us the revival of *Flora, the Red Menace*. We didn't solicit it.

KANDER: That was Scott's idea, and he introduced us to David and Susan. They are now part of this theater family that we've built up.

EBB: It was a charming production in a small, intimate space.

KANDER: Hal came to see it, and I remember he said something very generous to the effect of "Maybe this is how we should have done it in the first place."

EBB: It was one of those experiences when you don't do it right the first time and you have a chance to do it over again. We fixed that show and that was the most rewarding part of it for me. We put quite a few of our songs back into the show.

KANDER: Tommy Thompson wrote a whole new book using the songs that we had cut.

EBB: He actually restored what we had written originally.

KANDER: We put back "The Kid Herself."

EBB: And "Keepin' It Hot," which was a tap-dancing number that Mr. Abbott cut.

KANDER: We put back some characters and created a new one.

EBB: And we wrote some new songs.

KANDER: The Communist character that Peter Frechette played was much stronger than it had been when Bob Dishy performed that role. The show was much closer to the spirit of the novel. I don't know that there was even a line of dialogue left from the old book.

EBB: I remember Sondheim came.

KANDER: Oh, he did. I don't remember that.

EBB: Yes, he sat in the very first row, and it was a very small theater. We had one scene where Peter Frechette was on a cot and he had a number, "Where Did Everybody Go?" The lyric was "You look as though you know, so why won't someone tell me." He was supposed to deliver that to the audience, and he turned to look and he stared right into Stephen's face. He was right there. I'll never forget that. Peter couldn't help himself and hesitated for a moment. Afterwards, Stephen said nothing. He didn't talk to us at the end and he didn't speak to anybody. I have no idea what he thought.

KANDER: I never heard that story. Veanne Cox, who was playing Liza's part, was really nervous. Veanne sings very well, but to have to sing that score in front of Liza one night when she came scared her to death. But Liza was terrific with her. Liza often goes out of her way like that just to make people feel good about themselves.

EBB: The production didn't go anywhere or get picked up, but it gave us a chance to see the show again.

KANDER: Some friendships started from there that continue to this day, and the show did well.

EBB: We created a little talk with that show.

KANDER: There were good reviews, but that was another love fest. Incidentally, the musical director of that show, David Pogue, was a pianist and a composer, and he also wrote the book *Macs for Dummies*. David taught me about computers, and he played the score for that show. He has a regular column in the *Times* computer section.

EBB: You know, I still use my Smith Corona. I've never written on a computer.

KANDER: You're scared of them. You're scared of electronic mechanical things.

EBB: I hate them.

KANDER: Computers are a tremendous help for notation in many ways. It's slightly shorter, but it also means you can save all the versions you've done. It used to be, like back when we first wrote *Flora*, I would just get finished copying down a whole arrangement for a song with ink or pencil, and you would call me in the country and say you had two lines that you wanted to change.

EBB: Funny you should mention that because we just finished a song and I had an idea for a change last night, a really good line. I hope you can accommodate me.

KANDER: Fine. The point is, in those days when you would say that, I would curse you —

EBB: Curse me?

KANDER: Because it meant that I would have to erase the

whole page and do it over. Now I just click it into the computer and save the old line in case I want to go back to it.

EBB: Curse me? Very nice. I'm grateful for computers, I just don't want to use them because it's true that I'm absolutely in terror of them.

KANDER: For some reason I've really always liked them. Maybe it goes back to when I was taking electric plugs apart when I was a little kid.

EBB: You look at those things and can figure them out. Not me.

KANDER: In terms of music writing, a score looks so much better on the computer than my handwriting or most composers' handwriting. There are also all kinds of side benefits. For instance, if you want to transpose a song from the key you wrote it in for a singer or for you, all you have to do is punch a button. It's automatic. There's another benefit when it comes to proofreading. When I put the music into the computer, I can play it back at any speed I want and can hear the mistakes I've made.

EBB: A lyric isn't all that big a deal. So you put it on a new piece of paper.

KANDER: It used to nauseate me when we wrote them out. My hand would start to cramp because we were writing everything longhand, essentially. I would get up and clean the entire house rather than face having to do it. Now it takes time but I enjoy the process. Other people feel differently. I have friends who love doing it longhand, who love their own notation, and it's beautiful notation.

EBB: I like the time it takes to type a lyric. You have to stop and think about it. I don't like electric typewriters particularly because they're too fast. I like the old way—you hunt and peck, and as you go along, you're editing yourself. Curse me?

●　●　●

Kander and Ebb again worked with Scott Ellis, David Thompson, and Susan Stroman on an Off-Broadway retrospective revue, *And the World Goes 'Round: The Songs of Kander and Ebb*. This anthology of twenty-two Kander and Ebb songs included numbers from their shows and movies as well as special material. The cast featured Bob Cuccioli, Karen Mason, Brenda Pressley, Jim Walton, and Karen Ziemba. Produced in association with Princeton's McCarter Theatre, the show opened at the Westside Theater on March 18, 1991, and ran for 408 performances.

● ○ ●

KANDER: We had such a good time on *Flora, the Red Menace* that Scott, Tommy, and Susan Stroman came to us with the idea for a revue. We gave them access to everything we had and they decided what songs they wanted to use. We didn't make those choices.

EBB: *And the World Goes 'Round* was a perfect experience, I thought. We did very little except contribute everything that we ever wrote. They did everything else as far as putting the show together and programming it.

KANDER: All we were was avuncular. They had staging concepts for just about everything.

EBB: Oh, it was a pleasure to look at. They were all songs that we had written, like "Colored Lights" from *The Rink*. "Maybe This Time." "Money." "Cabaret." "Kiss of the Spider Woman."

KANDER: And from *Woman of the Year*, "Sometimes a Day Goes By."

EBB: "I Don't Remember You" from *The Happy Time* was also in it. "Pain" was one of my favorite songs in the show, and we originally wrote that for Chita Rivera's act, which she did with four boys. The best of anything is based on truth, of course, and art is truth. Chita often said how painful dancing was. Dancers are always in some kind of pain because they work so hard and use so many parts of the body. I think that piece of material was true to that world exactly.

KANDER: It also included a sadistic choreographer who was based on Ron Field.

EBB: Or Jerry Robbins. It was like a little musical and was done originally at the Grand Finale at West Seventy-first Street.

KANDER: It was also done wonderfully by Gwen Verdon and Liza and Chita.

EBB: Oh, that was a terrific night they gave us at Avery Fisher Hall [*November 12, 1978*]. The three girls—Liza, Chita, and Gwen—performed "Pain" and tore the house down. Quite a few of our friends appeared in that show. It was to raise funds for AMDA, the American Musical and Dramatic Academy. It also was a tribute to us, but that was tough because again I have a problem being celebrated that way. I remember at the end, we went onstage and—

KANDER: Yes, we introduced our mothers. My mother got up and shyly sat down again, and your mother got up—

EBB: And she's still bowing today. My sisters Norma and Essie were pulling on her dress, telling her to sit down. My mother said, "I'll sit down when I'm good and ready!" That was a memorable night.

KANDER: We were both scared to death.

EBB: Oh yes, we always are. That was the first one of those events of any real size.

KANDER: I think it was the best of those occasions.

EBB: You'll never get better talent than that. Lenya sang for the last time.

KANDER: Jack Gilford was in it.

EBB: And Robert Goulet. I wish we had that night on tape.

KANDER: Something happened that prevented them from

taping it, so there is no record of that night. It's becoming clear to me that there are certain people—I don't want to say they're our actors—but they are actors that we have worked with a great deal and for whom we have enormous personal feelings. In that sense, ours is not the usual transient theatrical situation. I'm thinking of people like Deb Monk and Karen Ziemba, who were both in *Steel Pier*.

EBB: Chita is one of them too. If we had a repertory company, we would have a nucleus of people like that.

KANDER: If we were casting people who we're really fond of and want to be around, those people would be in it. Almost unconsciously, when we start a project, we start looking for roles for those people.

EBB: We've been around a long time. Liza's voice was always in my head, and if there was a part for her, I always wanted her to do it.

KANDER: Liza was a special case.

EBB: Because she was a star early on, so it wasn't like you could just throw her into something.

KANDER: Rob Marshall is one of ours also. We've worked with him a great deal since he started off in *Zorba*.

EBB: These are all people we like to have around.

KANDER: Not only are they talented, but they make you feel good to be working with them. We're all, I think, concerned with each other's lives, and that's great. We like working with people we know and like both onstage and behind the scenes. It's very incestuous. Friends like Liza, Chita, Susan, and Rob are like family for us. We go through their highs and lows with them and they go through ours.

EBB: They are exceptional friends and remarkable people as well. I don't know how often you find that—the talent and the humanity all in one. I'm a little leery of actors ordinarily, but they transcend that.

KANDER: These people have lasted with us. Karen Ziemba and Brent Barrett have known each other forever. I guess they met on *And the World Goes 'Round*, and they have great fondness for each other. That chemistry came out on the stage whenever they performed with each other.

EBB: I love just seeing two people onstage who I like so much.

KANDER: I went backstage after they did *The Pajama Game* together and the conductor, Rob Fisher, came out and said, "Our babies are up there." I knew what he meant. There are very few things more exciting for me than seeing people who we started off working with at the beginnings of their careers and over time watching them become more and more developed and mature and successful. That's a thrill. Maybe that's one of the things that age and experience give you. You really learn to surround yourself with people who are really talented.

EBB: Every musical really should be a mutual admiration society. You should be able to sit down and say, "Oh, we have a David Loud as our music director who I admire more than anyone, and there's an actor who I admire playing that role, and he admires the way that you write and the way the lyrics will sound." When everybody admires everybody, out of that, I think, can come real quality.

KANDER: I think that's absolutely right. When we speak of collaboration, it's not just collaboration with the director and choreographer. It's everybody.

EBB: Everybody. Stagehands who go out there and get a scene changed in a minute or fix a foul like that.

KANDER: Randy Graff did a reading yesterday for a workshop of *Curtains*. She got a laugh on a line that's always been in the first act, but it was funny in a way that it's never been before, just because she screamed it. That was her instinct. With all those talented people in the reading, I just sat there with my eyes blinking, thinking, *How did you do that? How did you come up with that in no time?* We mentioned David Loud. Patrick Vacciarello is the musical director on the other workshop we are doing. *The Skin of Our Teeth.* He is another one of those guys—I don't know how they do it.

EBB: You know what? When people are good at what they do, you never really know how they do it. I mean, I listen to you play the piano and say, "How do you do that?" Or take a director like Frank Galati, with whom we did *The Visit* recently at the Goodman Theater. How does he get the show to look that good, to be that clearly spoken and articulated in a way that we could only pray our material would be realized? How does someone do that with such little time and little space, and with an eleven-piece orchestra?

KANDER: But you do the same thing, Freddy. If there's a moment that needs to be filled in, you'll say, "Give me a minute," and five minutes later it's all there. It's all rhymed and makes sense.

EBB: It just happens. That explains it as much as it can be explained. I think that people like David Loud and Patrick Vacciarello are just incredible at what they do, and our great fortune is having them work with us.

● ○ ●

Kander and Ebb again teamed up with Scott Ellis, David Thompson, and Susan Stroman to stage *Steel Pier*, a fanciful tale about a 1933 dance marathon with a ghost as its romantic lead. The songwriters came up with a delightfully evocative score, conjuring the spirit of the era with lyrical refrains like "Things work out, you're sure to find, / When you leave the world behind"— sung with the female chorus dancing on the wing of a biplane. The cast included Gregory Harrison, Karen Ziemba, Daniel Mc-

Donald, and Debra Monk. As a book musical, this Kander-Ebb show ran up against a season of pop operas when it opened for its quick-to-close run on April 24, 1997. The *New York Times* reported that *Steel Pier* "reminds us that these two men represent the survival of a form of musical that no one else is writing today: filled with that youthful joy that doesn't believe in despair or death."

● ○ ●

KANDER: We had a wonderful experience working on *Steel Pier* until we got into the theater. I don't know exactly why things changed. As I recall, there was a certain amount of panicking and a certain distance from the show in the theater, whereas in the studio, we had been right on top of these people. It was very emotional and funny, and everybody's work was really good. The making of it was really a joy for me. We worked on that piece with Scott Ellis, David Thompson, and Susan Stroman, and the five of us sat around playing "What if?" forever.

EBB: I remember we wrote "Running in Place" very late while we were already in previews for *Steel Pier*.

KANDER: The idea there was to try and make a big dance moment for Karen Ziemba, and Susan did a terrific job choreographing that scene.

EBB: The critics attacked that piece like we were getting arty at the end. We didn't seem to be able to do anything right with *Steel Pier*. They weren't having it.

KANDER: I think "First You Dream" is as good a lyrical moment, romantic moment, as we've ever written. It's almost a perfect lyric, perfect song. There was a story there. The marathons would sometimes develop for the audience's delight a love relationship for a couple of those poor, tired marathon dancers. Then they would have a wedding with a tent, so the newly married couple could be alone together. In *Steel Pier*, the heroine, Rita, has a date with an exhibition pilot, but his plane crashes. He's allowed to come back to the world to be with her for a short period of time. We were thinking of the Orpheus myth when we wrote the song, which he sings to her in the tent. The conceit is that she sees what he sees while he sings to her, so she is flying with him. He tells her not to look back, and for a long time, she doesn't. But finally she does look and that brings them back to earth. You may not buy this, Freddy, but I've always felt that if she hadn't looked, when they pulled the tent away, the couple would have been gone:

Bill:
First you dream,
Dream about incredible things
Then you look
And suddenly you have wings.
You can fly,
You can fly
But first you dream.

First you dream,
Dream about remarkable times
Close your eyes
And see how your spirit climbs.
You can fly
You can soar
Feel the wind
Hear it roar
It's easy now
Imagine that
But first you dream.

Rita and Bill:
Here we are
High above the rooftops.
There's a barn
There's a field of corn
And that little white house
Where another you was born.
Isn't it fine?
Isn't it fair,
Being up here
Looking down there?

Bill:
Take my hand,
I promise that I won't let you fall.
Don't look back,
The looking back could end it all.
Off we go
To the sky
Straight ahead
You and I
Together now
Together now
But first things first:
First you dream.

EBB: I thought it worked, and I think "Everybody's Girl" was a good comic song.

KANDER: That was one of those shows where it was the people that made it so special, in some ways, the casting itself. Our friendship with Debra Monk, which is now very strong, certainly began with *Steel Pier*. And Daniel McDonald became a very close friend and got married in my house out in the country.

Karen Ziemba had been part of our life before, with *And the World Goes 'Round*, and we hope that continues. David Loud, the music director, was also part of *World Goes 'Round*, and he is music director of our new show, *The Visit*.

KANDER: But that whole year with the workshop and rehearsals, every time I walked through the door of that rehearsal room I looked forward to it because there wasn't a single person in the room that I wasn't really happy to see. I think everybody felt that way.

EBB: I remember that we had trouble with the opening number, which we wrote first and was never really right. "Willing to Ride (Here I Go Again)." The audience didn't really get into it as much as I would have liked. But it's all perception. My perception of the number was that it should have made the audience more responsive. The reception was respectful but the song never got an enormous hand.

KANDER: It wasn't the best song in the show.

EBB: I didn't know how to fix it.

KANDER: There was one thing that hurt us, though I don't mean this is the reason the show failed. At the beginning of the show, the pilot, played by Daniel McDonald, sort of rose up and went offstage without explanation. That confused people, and then we got a lot of advice from people who suggested that we had to have an airplane crash and we had to see the pilot with his jacket burning. Then the show became more and more and more literal, so the whole thing turned into *Touched by an Angel*, which was a big mistake.

EBB: I think they thought it was silly having this dead guy as the hero.

KANDER: That was perfectly obvious.

EBB: It was the wrong show at the wrong time. It was done differently later, when they cut that whole beginning and just told the story straightforwardly.

KANDER: But you shouldn't find out that he's dead until the second act when the girl, his partner in the marathon, finds out.

EBB: It worked much better without that business at the beginning.

KANDER: There was panic going on about how the audience doesn't understand the beginning of the show and we have to make it clearer. Still, there was something else, and I don't know if it was the set or our mistakes, but there was an emotional distance in the theater that was not there in the studio.

EBB: We never connected with the audience, really, except a little bit with her song, but there wasn't a hell of a lot of reaction. I thought Susan's dances were wonderful. My God, she staged a jitterbug that was fabulous, but the audiences seemed to overlook the miraculous pieces like that.

KANDER: When we were in the big studio and had bleachers up and small audiences, there was great enthusiasm and everybody would be in tears at the end.

EBB: You know what happened, we had to manufacture a story to accommodate that dance marathon milieu. We really wanted to do *They Shoot Horses, Don't They?* and when we couldn't get the rights to do that, we kept the marathon idea and constructed the story around that. I guess the effort looked a little desperate. I don't have a hell of a lot of affection for that show.

KANDER: Oh, I do, and I have terrific affection for those characters. The love story moved me tremendously.

EBB: I wasn't moved. You are way more romantic than I am. I appreciated it, and I loved my collaborators and the cast. Everything you're supposed to love, I loved. But I don't think the show ever worked, and I don't completely disagree with the criticism that was leveled at it for being slight, though it was powerful-looking. I watched the ending of the first act every day because I loved it so. What was it called?

KANDER: That was the sprint.

EBB: All of them ran around in a circle. It was a custom in a marathon and I just loved that we put that on the stage.

KANDER: There was an emotional moment in that piece that really killed me every time, when Daniel McDonald as the pilot doesn't know that he's dead. He's just finding this out, and the girl who he's in love with has fallen down. Suddenly, he just instinctively puts his hand up—

EBB: During the sprint.

KANDER: And everybody stops. He looks at his hand and realizes that he has that kind of power to be able to do that—I mean, I'll get teary just describing this, believe me. Then slowly he got everybody to move back several bars of music.

EBB: They moved in reverse.

KANDER: We played the music in reverse, and they very slowly went back. Then he let his hand go again, and everybody picked up where they left off, and she made it. It was the moment of recognition, and I bawled like a baby every time.

EBB: The sprint was Susan and Scott at their best.

KANDER: The show had a marvelous cast.

EBB: And a wonderful libretto idea.

KANDER: I felt differently than you about *They Shoot Horses, Don't They?* It seemed obvious that we should try to get the rights, but it's a story which has always seemed to me a bit unrealistically dark and bleak.

EBB: So you went for a ghost story where a dead man comes back! Unrealistic?

KANDER: I mean emotionally unrealistic.

EBB: I thought it was terrific.

KANDER: They researched and had speakers come who had been in marathons, and the fact is those marathons were not these terribly dark, bleak, desperate things. There were people who were there to get their moment in the sun.

EBB: But that was the movie's take on it.

KANDER: And also the novel's take on it.

EBB: I liked that. I thought there was an element that was desperate and hideous, the exploitation of people to win a couple of bucks if they could stay on their feet. We tried to get the rights because the story really intrigued David and me and Scott and Susan. I didn't know you didn't care for it.

KANDER: I wasn't going to object to it. I loved the idea of the milieu. There was a kind of Kansas City jazz that I was aware of growing up, and when we wrote *Steel Pier* I found myself going back and listening to some of those recordings to just absorb that sound and atmosphere from the thirties. My grandparents took me to Atlantic City when I was six, the same year that *Steel Pier* takes place, 1933.

EBB: When the rights to *They Shoot Horses* weren't available, we started on our own libretto.

KANDER: This was another project that evolved the way that *And the World Goes 'Round* did, with Scott, Susan, and Tommy. We loved them, and then we wanted to be together again.

EBB: I would do it again tomorrow.

KANDER: You bet.

EBB: I love them, and I think they're wildly gifted. I would be very happy and proud to work with them again. But that has nothing to do with my opinion of *Steel Pier*. Because everybody did their job.

KANDER: You're right, even with our differences of opinion. But the romantic element of that piece thrilled me.

EBB: Ugh.

KANDER: We should have stage directions: *Fred sticks finger down throat.*

EBB: [*laughing*] *John bangs on table and screams.*

KANDER: Actually, *Steel Pier* and *The Rink* were connected in that both of those shows were terribly emotional experiences for us.

EBB: I remember having the highest hopes for them and then being unfulfilled emotionally. I don't remember going into any of the others with the kind of high expectation that we had for them. They were our two biggest disappointments, weren't they?

KANDER: Yes, no question.

EBB: Not because they failed, but because of how much I loved them.

KANDER: That's exactly the way I feel. I could watch them over and over. We both used to go back to see them again. Both of the shows deal with personal emotions; they were not political statements.

EBB: They were not dark or tough.

KANDER: They were more about people than any two shows we have ever done.

EBB: They were crushing because we had such high hopes dashed. You know the line "They had it coming" from *Chicago*. But I never saw it coming with *The Rink* or *Steel Pier*.

KANDER: My memory is that even though I liked the scores of both shows, it was those characters and the actors we had playing them that made them such special experiences. I thought our work on both of those shows was really good, but for me it wasn't about the recognition of skill so much as it was rejecting the big emotional investment that we both had. The *Steel Pier* cast was much larger than that of *The Rink*, but in both shows the companies were terribly caring, terribly committed. At the end of *Steel Pier*, there was a moment that Karen Ziemba and Daniel McDonald had, where they just hold each other and the music swells and he goes away. That's another one of those moments that even to this day if I think of it, I start to tear up. There was just no way not to be moved by that moment. More than just the love story, the *Steel Pier* is about a lot of people who are living in a difficult time, the Depression, and who are trying to survive by any means that they can. Some of them do and some of them don't, and many of them are trying to survive in the wrong way. They've been sold a kind of show-business dream with the marathon. Oh, God, I remember how moved I was when I saw Deb Monk sitting there and singing the song "Somebody Older" when she's trying to talk this young man into taking her away with him.

EBB: *Steel Pier* was also very emotional for me. I cared about the people in it enormously. Deb Monk, Karen Ziemba, Danny McDonald. They were very dear and the rehearsal period was very special. I was sorry when we opened—I wish we could have just rehearsed.

KANDER: I felt the same.

EBB: I thought the dancing in *Steel Pier* was about as good as any dancing I had seen. Oddly enough, with the Tonys that year we lost to ourselves, because *Steel Pier* lost to the revival of *Chicago*. Ann Reinking won over Susan Stroman. I thought that was unfortunate, as much as I love Ann and loved seeing *Chicago* get yet another award. I was sorry Susan wasn't recognized for that extraordinary work she did.

KANDER: *Steel Pier* was about dancing. There wasn't a moment in it when there wasn't movement.

EBB: Gregory Harrison was wonderful. That may have been the first time he did a musical, but he was terrific.

KANDER: Both shows, I think, broke our hearts.

EBB: You might think that anything that fails breaks your heart, but that's not true.

KANDER: No, not true.

EBB: It has to be beyond that. *Flora, the Red Menace* didn't break my heart in the same way.

KANDER: In both of those shows we had big emotional

investments, and if somebody asked if you could go back and relive an experience in one of your shows, it would be *Steel Pier* or *The Rink*. I would want to go back and live through the whole thing just as it was, not go back and do something different.

NINE

Chicago, the Movie

The screen version of *Chicago* waited more than twenty-five years to be made. Directed by Rob Marshall and written by Bill Condon, the movie was released on December 27, 2002, with a cast that featured Catherine Zeta-Jones (Velma), Renée Zellweger (Roxie), Richard Gere (Billy Flynn), Queen Latifah (Mama Morton), and John C. Reilly (Amos "Mr. Cellophane" Hart). The movie won six Academy Awards, including Best Picture and Best Supporting Actress for Catherine Zeta-Jones. Thanks to the movie's enormous popularity, the soundtrack became a surprise hit for Sony's Epic label.

●　●　●

EBB: Nobody wanted to make the movie of *Chicago* for a long time.

KANDER: I remember the subject of the movie came up the last time I saw Fosse. You were in California, and Bobby and I went to Hugh Wheeler's funeral here. Bobby had not been able to figure out how to do the film. But after the funeral reception, he told me, "I think I finally figured out how to do the movie, and when Fred gets back, we'll talk about it." It was the first time he ever said that, and that was the last that I ever saw of him. He died shortly after that. What his version of the movie would have been like we will never know, because he never told anyone.

E BB : I didn't have a clue how to do the movie.

K AN DE R : It also took a long time before anybody wanted to do the movie of *Cabaret*, and it sold for very little, as I recall.

E BB : So did *Chicago*.

K AN DE R : The cast is really wonderful, and you know I'm kind of a snob about people who are primarily movie stars. When I saw how talented they are—Catherine Zeta-Jones, Renée Zellweger, and Richard Gere—I was ashamed of myself because they are all extremely gifted. They could step right into the show. Richard Gere could play Billy Flynn like that! [*snapping fingers*]

E BB : And he would have an affection for it. They all have special feelings for the piece, and that is gratifying. We had the opportunity to meet the whole company when they were filming in Toronto last year. They are a terrific group of people and they treated us like royalty. We heard Renée Zellweger sing "Funny Honey" and "Nowadays." John C. Reilly sang "Mr. Cellophane," and Richard Gere sang "All I Care About Is Love" and "Razzle Dazzle." Catherine Zeta-Jones sang "All That Jazz." I added a line to "Class" for the movie. It was actually the first line that I ever wrote for the song, but Bobby Fosse thought it was too much, so we cut it. The line in the show eventually became "Everybody you watch / S'got his brain in his crotch." But I put back in the original line, which was "Every guy is a snot, every girl is a twat." By the way, we scarcely have any money participation in the movie.

K AN DE R : They have to pay us for a new song, though practically nothing.

E BB : I think we were lucky to get *Chicago* done at all. Nobody wanted it. I tell you, Marty Richards persevered. He produced the show and hung on to it and believed in it. He kept trying to get it done as a movie.

K AN DE R : At one point when we were working on the movie of *New York, New York*, you and I and Liza together went to Scorsese and asked him to do it. I don't know if he ever seriously considered it or not. I'm glad the movie has turned out the way it has, and we are both grateful that Rob Marshall directed it.

E B B : I can name quite a few people who have come and gone on that project. Fosse and Madonna. Rob Iscove. Then there were people like Nicholas Hytner and Wendy Wasserstein. They had written a script for it. Nick Hytner had shopped it around Hollywood with him directing and Charlize Theron to star in it. But nobody picked it up. At one point, Liza and Goldie Hawn wanted to do the movie. Liza was going to be Roxie, and Goldie was going to be Velma. They even sang "All That Jazz" at the end of the TV special that I did with them, *Goldie and Liza Together*. They had a wonderful friendship for a while.

K A N D E R : Larry Gelbart also wrote a screenplay for *Chicago*. He was paid a lot of money for that.

E B B : They kept sending him back to rewrite it until eventually he said, "Enough." Apparently at Miramax there are a lot of young people out of college and they read scripts for Harvey Weinstein and the producers. They have meetings, one of which I went to with Larry. A young guy who looked like a Harvard undergraduate came in and started to attack Larry's screenplay, but he did so for ridiculous reasons. He suggested that Roxie has to have a love affair. "You cannot do a major musical without a love affair," he insisted. He referred to the movie of *Roxie Hart* and pointed out how well that was handled, that Ginger Rogers had a love affair with a reporter. Then he said to Larry, "So why don't you write in a reporter who's covering the case and have him get involved with Roxie." That kind of advice is insulting for somebody as gifted and important as Larry, though he took it very well. I kept kicking him under the table.

K A N D E R : I think he's been through that kind of shit many times. In the theater you own your own material, and nobody can tell you that you have to change something. They can try to pressure you, but with movies you are just for hire. That's why Larry is so expensive. He gets the money up front, writes the script, and if they give him too much of a hassle, he can just say, "The hell with it."

EBB: The idea of seeing the story through Roxie's eyes is a wonderful idea.

KANDER: That was Rob Marshall's idea. Suggesting that concept was how he got the job.

EBB: Yes, he pitched it to Miramax.

KANDER: As I understand it, they were talking to him about doing *Rent*, and basically he said, "Before we talk about that, I'd like to talk about *Chicago*." He had this idea, and whatever he said got him the job.

EBB: It's extraordinary with a $45 million movie for some-one to get the job based on saying, "We're going to see the story through Roxie's eyes." Rob had so little experience with movies.

KANDER: He did that TV movie of *Annie*.

EBB: The movie of *Chicago* is a wildly improbable success story. Good for him! Good for us!

KANDER: The most amazing thing in this whole experience is Rob, particularly when somebody you know as long and as well as we have known him. To see somebody that we're that close to go off and do something so wildly different.

EBB: It's so improbable that it could be the basis for another movie.

KANDER: This sort of thing happened to me once before. Years ago I knew an actor-singer named Kenneth Nelson, who was known for doing musicals. He had a beautiful voice. He had been a very close friend for a number of years and then I went to see *Boys in the Band*. Suddenly there was somebody who I thought I knew vomiting his guts out on the stage giving such a performance that when I went back to see him afterwards, I felt really shy. I realized I didn't know that person as well as I thought

I did, and I think we did not know Rob as well as we thought. His contribution codirecting *Cabaret* was enormous and he also saved us with *Kiss of the Spider Woman*, where he was choreographer. But film is a different medium. Where do you learn to say "Cut" or "Action"? That's what I'm talking about.

EBB: It's a whole different ball of wax, not just dancing. How did Rob get those performances in *Chicago*? How does he know so much?

KANDER: The most amazing thing is that he sat down and worked out on paper every one of those scenes. So that was no accident—

EBB: I can't begin to imagine how difficult that must be, and he choreographed it. He did everything. He coordinated all of that with what it looks like and how it's lit.

KANDER: With the movie of *Cabaret*, Fosse went way far afield from the original stage production in order to make a movie. He really changed the dramatic focus. It was wonderful, though the first time we saw it, we didn't think so.

EBB: I thought he messed it up.

KANDER: But the second time we saw it, we both thought it was a masterpiece. I think the first time we were simply not prepared for how different it was from the original.

EBB: Cy Feuer showed *Cabaret* to us in California. He said, "Don't pay any attention to it. It's rough. The sound is off." When it was over, I complained about everything that I was told to ignore. I thought her speech at the end about not going to London was ridiculous. I was just really petulant and argumentative. I thought they had ruined it, but then I saw it again with Liza at the Ziegfeld and with an audience that was loving it. That helped.

KANDER: *Chicago*, the movie, is much closer to the original intention of the piece than the movie of *Cabaret* was. *Cabaret* is a marvelous piece of moviemaking, you could almost say *suggested* by the stage piece. The *Chicago* movie is much closer to the stage piece. That doesn't make one better than the other. They are just different. I think the opening of the movie from Roxie's point of view is fantastic and makes the whole movie work. I'm so glad they did it. That makes me so happy. It's not intended to be a realistic piece. That opening is the core of the story. Moment by moment, it's not literal in the stage piece and it's not literal in the film. If it had been literal or realistic that way, I think the story would have been boring. The thing that I like about the film, the thing that is more personally satisfying to me than *Cabaret*, is that in order to do *Cabaret* Fosse had to go all over the place and change the story radically, and the focus of the piece. He took out a great deal of the music. It was like starting all over with the same raw material.

What was brilliant about what Rob did, I thought, was that he came up with a very clear and simple solution which allowed him to do the stage piece, and yet it was a movie, very much a movie movie. It was as if he were doing both a stage piece and a movie at the same time. I thought that was most ingenious, capturing the feeling of a stage piece in a movie. Rob's choreography accomplished the same thing that Fosse's did in the show but Rob was very careful not to ape Bobby's style. I think he succeeded very well. There is so much editing in the film to keep it as a film that you don't get long stretches of uninterrupted dance. If a dance goes on all the way through a number, there is a lot of cutting away, which is what makes it a movie. Even though there is a lot of dancing going on, you never feel that you're an audience member in a theater watching a stage number, except toward the end, when he does "Hot Honey Rag." Even then there are little touches that keep it from falling into that trap. The biggest thing about it is that he manages to capture the feeling of the stage piece in a movie.

E B B : The whole reaction to the movie of *Chicago* and the soundtrack has been overwhelming. We've never experienced anything like this before, and we never expected it.

KANDER: I don't think it was anticipated by Miramax either, or by Sony.

EBB: Miramax kept hedging their bets. They put a song we didn't write called "Love Is a Crime" on the soundtrack to attract a younger audience with an artist named Anastacia. They didn't feel our music would attract enough young people to buy the album.

KANDER: That song is on the soundtrack only because we legally could not stop it. We were able to stop them from putting the song in the film. They wanted to have it play with the credits of the film. Our lawyers were able to prevent that. Harvey Weinstein, who runs Miramax, apparently wanted music that would appeal to sixteen-year-olds.

EBB: He must have thought the project's appeal with our score was to middle-age and older-age audiences. He also hired Janet Jackson to write another song, thinking that she would attract a younger audience.

KANDER: She was paid $300,000 to write a song. Clearly, Sony and Harvey Weinstein have no confidence in our score, or very little. I think we should tell this story. Apparently, Janet Jackson actually did write something and apparently it was terrible, though we have never heard it. I found out about her being hired to write a song only because my friend Albert was online and he saw this story about Janet Jackson being contracted to write a song.

EBB: We would never have known if he hadn't ran across the story.

KANDER: I came home from a concert one night, and there on my pillow was a printout of the story. You know how certain things happen, and at the time you're really frustrated because you can't do anything about it. It was late at night when I found out so there was nobody I could call. I knew, or at least I was fairly sure, that we had an ironclad clause in our contract, which indeed we did, protecting the integrity of the piece. So the next morning I got ahold of our agents, Sam Cohn and Maarten Kooij, and they went to Miramax. The first response was that Harvey wanted to talk to us about this. We both said no. Neither of us wanted to meet with Harvey. They came back to us a number of times, and then I got a call at my house in the country from Marty Richards saying that Harvey wanted him to ask us if we would consider collaborating on a song with Janet Jackson.

EBB: [*laughing*] That might have been fun, huh?

KANDER: Of course we said no. We kept getting these requests from Harvey to meet with us because I guess Harvey feels he can talk anybody into anything. We continued to say no. Sam Cohn, who was chortling with joy at this point, called back to tell Harvey no, and he reached Harvey's second-in-command or assistant. Sam said, "No, the guys do not want to meet with Harvey." This is like the definition of what happens with a powerful one-man organization like Miramax. The response was a tremulous "Well, Harvey's not going to like that." But we were finally able to prevent anyone else's song from being in the credits.

EBB: Being played over the credits can make a song eligible for an Academy Award nomination. This is a new rule. Even though it's not in the body of the picture, if an original song plays over the end credits, it is eligible. None of our other songs were eligible, because they were already in the stage version.

KANDER: Yes, they decided that they wanted a new song especially for the movie, to play over the credits so they would have something for Academy Award consideration. I have two words for that: Ha! But we did write a new song, "I Move On," at the request of the director, Rob Marshall, and the screenwriter, Bill Condon, to replace the song "Nowadays."

EBB: Or, actually, to come after "Nowadays" and run over the credits. Then they wanted "I Move On" to end the movie.

KANDER: It was a last-minute scramble because they wasted so much time trying to talk us into sitting around the kitchen table with Janet Jackson. Originally, the bows in the movie were taken over the overture. When it turned out that for a song to be eligible for an Oscar it had to be the first thing that you hear after the movie is over, I had to write an orchestral piece for the bows based on the song "I Move On." You would have to listen very carefully to know that the final piece is based on that song that runs over the credits, but it is and that is what makes it eligible. I don't think we actually have a prayer to get an Academy Award, for a good reason. Harvey is going to push hard for the song by U2 from *Gangs of New York*, which Miramax also produced. For the same reason I would be very surprised if Rob Marshall gets an Academy Award because Harvey is going to push hard for Scorsese. That's a hundred-million-plus movie, and not a particularly well-received film, so Harvey is going to fight for that one to get the directing and original-song awards. *Chicago* cost about half as much as *Gangs* to make. A lot of this has to do with Hollywood politics and tells you a little bit about that mentality. I don't think of it as malicious. What they did may be stupid and tasteless, but I don't think they were doing it to say, "Now we're going to do this with the music, and the songwriters are going to be miserable."

EBB: It had nothing to do with Kander and Ebb. It was all about marketing and selling a movie that cost millions of dollars. Behind the scenes it was a very complicated, terrible story and a great pity that the whole thing happened, between Janet Jackson and even our credit at the end of the movie. Originally, we were not high in the credits. Music and lyrics appeared far down on the list. That was a struggle to have changed. The lovely part for us now is that the movie is being recognized and is so well received, and for that we can only be wildly grateful. But the way the song was treated and the way we were treated personally—that was not a pleasant experience.

KANDER: We weren't badly treated so much as not treated. The best thing about it was that both Rob and Bill Condon were very solicitous about our feelings as far as the direction and writing.

EBB: They were both perfect gentlemen. Everything in the movie besides "I Move On" was also in the show. But there are songs in the show like "Class" that are not in the movie. "A Little Bit of Good" and "My Own Best Friend" were also left out of the movie.

KANDER: Every song that's not there in the movie is not there for a dramatic reason. There was no other consideration. After all their push to have us write a song for sixteen-year-olds, it turns out that "All That Jazz" has become so popular that they are releasing that song as the single. For some reason, this album has skyrocketed.

EBB: It's been quite extraordinary in every way. If you were looking to have a last laugh, here it is. But I'm getting surprisingly little satisfaction. I'm delighted but it's been so hard and tough. I'm not enjoying it as much.

KANDER: We differ on that a little. I get more fun out of it than you do. I'm conditioned to get more fun out of things than you are. When Albert and I were on our way to Washington to be with Chita for her Kennedy Center Honor last year, we arrived the night before, and I had been saying on the plane that at least we were going to be away from any telephone calls from Miramax. After arriving, I went into the shower, and when I came out there were two calls from Miramax and one from Sam Cohn about this soundtrack song.

"Love Is a Crime" sung by Anastacia went on the soundtrack even though it's not in the movie. That's what those calls were about, to let us know that even with our refusal to allow the song on the soundtrack, they were going to go ahead and include it anyway. Finally, when I called Sam back, I asked the crucial question: "Is there anything that we can do legally to stop it?" He said, "No," and at that point, we realized that we had done our best and couldn't prevent it from happening, so we let it go. I think Harvey had made a commitment to the guy that was running Sony at the time to allow them to use this song on the album. His name was Tommy Mottola. I think a lot of the monetary support came from Sony, and when this happened with the soundtrack, I think almost immediately Tommy Mottola was let go from Sony. So the person to whom Harvey had made the commitment was no longer in charge of Sony. It was all very baroque.

EBB: I am thrilled to hear about the record hitting the charts, but I don't have the kind of joy I would have had otherwise if all this hadn't happened along the way. But it did happen and I don't have the charity in me to forget it. I mean, there were endless phone calls just to have our names appear where they should have been in the first place. Our position came down to what Miramax was required to do to acknowledge the music in the credits. We were in the twenty-eighth position on the end credit. We fought and fought and eventually moved up to twelve. Words and music in a movie musical like that where so much of it is the score? There was too much anguish for me to get over it easily.

KANDER: One of the great joys with the success of this movie for me goes back to the original reception for *Chicago*, which was critically mixed, if anything. The fact that the piece has made its journey relatively intact over twenty-seven years to a point where it has suddenly become such a phenomenon, I think that's delicious.

EBB: It's astonishing. You know what's funny, I rarely buy or read *The New Yorker*, but at Christmas I received a subscription, and the very first issue that came had the review of the movie, and it was one of the very few bad reviews. I happen to think it was an idiotic review written by a man who didn't seem to know his ass from his elbow. But it was a bad review nevertheless.

KANDER: One of the other bad reviews of the movie was in

Variety, and it reminded me of the original review in *Variety* of *Cabaret* on the stage, part of which I committed to memory: "It is unlikely there will be much of an audience for this sort of thing."

EBB: Reviews like that are kind of notorious, aren't they? They are history-making when they're so wrong. The longer I live, the more convinced I am that you just have to get over things, when things go wrong or people disappoint you. You need to get over bad reviews. As Cher said when she slapped Nicolas Cage's face in *Moonstruck*, "Snap out of it!"

KANDER: That was a marvelous moment, and just when he said, "I love you."

EBB: You get over death, you get over love, and you go on. Listen to me. [*laughing*] I'm the old philosopher now.

TEN

Colored Lights

Recently, Kander and Ebb contributed new songs to Liza Minnelli's comeback tour and to a workshop for a new musical, *Curtains*, undertaken for the Nederlander Organization. This show was written by Peter Stone and is being directed by Scott Ellis. The songwriters also worked on regional tryouts of *Over & Over* (Joseph Stein's adaptation of Thornton Wilder's *The Skin of Our Teeth*) and *The Visit* (Terrence McNally's adaptation of Friedrich Dürrenmatt's play). Directed by Frank Galati and starring Chita Rivera, *The Visit* received encouraging notices during its run at Chicago's Goodman Theater in the fall of 2001.

The Visit had originally been scheduled to open on Broadway the year before with Angela Lansbury in the lead, but the star had to withdraw because of her husband's failing health. It was then scheduled to open with Chita Rivera at the Public Theater in New York early in 2004, but that run was also delayed. At the time that Kander and Ebb conversed about this project and the current state of Broadway, they had not yet been able to find a theater for the show. The musical was at first considered too dark to be commercial. A macabre comedy of revenge, the book tells the story of Claire Zachanassian, the wealthiest woman in the world, who returns to her hometown after many years and tempts the impoverished townspeople with an offer of money for the murder of a man who once disgraced her.

• • •

EBB: Nobody wanted to do *The Visit* after Angela Lansbury left. The producer, Barry Brown, had raised eight and a half million dollars on Angela's name, so we had to replace Angela with a name of similar stature. Glenn Close turned us down and Judi Dench couldn't do it. It turned out that Shirley MacLaine also had a conflict, though she was interested at first. Years ago I worked on the TV special *Gypsy in My Soul* with Shirley more or less by myself. You weren't directly involved in that show.

KANDER: No, I wasn't. You liked Shirley, didn't you?

EBB: I thought she and the show were terrific. She was funny. She was real and genuine. She embraced the gypsies on the show, and they loved her. It was a joy to work with Shirley, and we laughed incessantly. For reasons I don't remember, she started calling me "My Little Something." She would say, "Hello, Little Something," and I knew that was me.

Shirley kept in touch with me over the years, and when we were first working on *The Visit* and Angela Lansbury decided not to do it, Shirley somehow got hold of the script. Obviously, she was offered the part, but you and I knew nothing about that until she called and left me a message saying, "Little Something, you've done it again. *The Visit* is a masterpiece." I kept the tape so I would always have that recording. She went on to say, "This show is brilliant. It's marvelous. It creates a terrific problem in my life because in order to do it I'll have to give up some other projects I had planned on doing, but it will probably be worth it because the show is just great. Can I meet with you?"

We both happened to be in California. So I called her back and we went to dinner, a Chinese meal in Beverly Hills. She was all into this project. She knew that we didn't quite have the money yet, and now that Angela was not doing it, raising the money might be a problem. Of course, Shirley knew that if she did it we could raise that money overnight. I told her I thought the best thing she could do was come to New York to meet the director, Frank Galati, and the writer, Terrence McNally. She agreed that she would come to New York, and we parted that night wonderful friends, hugging and kissing in my driveway.

Now a week passes. The Democratic Convention came to Los Angeles, and Shirley was all over the papers. She was at all the meetings, all the rallies and fund-raisers, but nowhere was there any indication that she would be going to New York. In the meantime, I had told our producer that I thought she was going to do the show, and naturally we were thrilled because Shirley's name would generate the money for us. At last a phone call came. She told me, "Fred, two projects—not one but two—with which I have been involved have finally found financing and are go projects. I feel that since I developed them with the writers, I owe it to them to stay here and work on these projects. So I'll have to pass on *The Visit*." I thought that was such a capricious change of heart. But as it turned out later, you said that you were not in favor of casting Shirley anyway.

KANDER: I just didn't think she was right for the role.

EBB: She might or might not have been good in the part. I guess we will never know now.

KANDER: It would have been a different show. I remember meeting her once—was it at your house or Liza's house?

EBB: Mine.

KANDER: You introduced us, and Shirley looked me up and down and said, "You're not in show business, are you?" I didn't know what to say at first. I sort of understood what she meant, and I said, "I guess not." She was perfectly pleasant, but she had me sized me up really fast. To paint a different kind of star picture, after working with Angela Lansbury on *The Visit*, I think Angie is one of the greatest people I've ever met. None of that big deal attitude, nothing even remotely flaky. We had a splendid time with her, and then her reason for not doing the show in the end was the best reason in the world.

EBB: I couldn't agree with you more.

KANDER: Her husband, Peter Shaw, was very ill and they had been married more than fifty years. She was not going to allow herself to be away from him for more than two weeks.

EBB: I supported that move, but at the same time my heart was breaking. I still think she did the right thing.

KANDER: During our weeks with her, there was not a single moment of "I can do whatever I want."

EBB: I never experienced that with Shirley either. I adore her, but I was disappointed in the way she dropped the project.

KANDER: I was relieved. We were going to have a star-controlled show, and that made me not look forward to it.

EBB: But everything has worked out for the best.

KANDER: Chita Rivera is the definition of Claire in *The Visit*. She is the perfect person to play that role. We started this project before Angie was involved, and in my mind it was never a piece that was being written specifically for her. Not that she's not a terrific lady or wouldn't have been wonderful. There were three people that I always thought could really play the part. One was Angie, one was Judi Dench, and one was Chita. I still feel that way. Glenn Close was talked about, and I heard names of other people who were approached, people who I thought were all wrong for it. As far as I'm concerned, we got one of my top three performers and nobody will ever be better in this part than Chita. She gives the performance of a lifetime.

EBB: Oh, it was bliss working with Chita, and she gives as good a performance as I've ever seen her give. The production at the Goodman Theater was a lovely experience for us even though the World Trade Center disaster happened while we were in Chicago and during that time I was going in and out of the hospital. But the show was terrific and the direction flawless. It is a show where whether it works now or not—which we are about to find out—you can have no regrets. You can't look back and say—

KANDER: Somebody did us in. Nobody's doing us in on this show.

EBB: No, not a gripe in the world from me. We've waited and now we're coming in with what may be a truly sterling production. It will be up there, and if they like it, they like it. But the theater has changed so much that producers can't take the kind of chances that were once taken with us. *Flora* was a big flop, and I doubt that if today we wrote a *Flora* we could then bounce into a *Cabaret*. We will get on with *The Visit*, but we still have to wait in line, and if Billy Joel comes up with a rock musical, he may get a theater before us.*

KANDER: It may take us longer to get a show on these days—

EBB: How much longer can it take? My God, it's already been two years. I had wanted to come right in.

KANDER: Being impatient is one thing.

EBB: [*laughing*] Another one of my virtues.

KANDER: Considering the way Broadway is today, I have to agree with Steve Sondheim when he says that *The Lion King* is not a show that makes him want to write. I don't go to see *The Lion King* and then suddenly find I can't wait to dash home to work with you.

EBB: No, not like when you went to see *Pajama Game* and you wanted to write like Adler and Ross, or you saw *Guys and Dolls* and you wanted nothing more in the world than to write like Frank Loesser.

*Ebb's speculation turned out to be prophetic, as this conversation took place more than nine months before the Billy Joel–Twyla Tharp show, *Movin' Out*, opened at the Richard Rodgers Theater on October 24, 2002.

KANDER: Or *Forum*. I don't despair about the changes on Broadway the way that Steve does because I think some people from our generation are still writing, along with younger new talents, and there is room for all of us. However, I think more than anything else the financial character of Broadway has changed to such an extent that it's only the most commercial kind of enterprise that can get on, like when you have people who have as much money as Disney has. I hadn't thought about it until now, but if *Cabaret* were a brand-new show and if Hal wanted to do it today, even with all his clout he would have a terrible time getting it on.

EBB: You know what I miss? The atmosphere of working in the theater as it used to be. For the most part, that's gone. There is more tension now and enormous pressure to succeed.

KANDER: I think that is true not so much in rehearsal but in the business of the theater. When we started working with Hal and Mr. Abbott, a musical could open for $150,000, play a year, and make its money back. Everything didn't have to be an event and there were producers who actually produced. It used to be that there were a lot of tryout cities for shows that were bound for Broadway. New Haven. Boston. Atlantic City during the thirties. It's a different system now. Almost everything that comes to Broadway these days has been done first at either a regional theater or an Off-Broadway house, rather than starting out as a production on the road destined for Broadway that goes to several cities.

EBB: The mechanics of getting a show on is entirely different now, as is raising money.

KANDER: There's a big difference between the two systems. When you did a show that was destined for Broadway, you did the production that would go into a Broadway house, and you would play in relatively Broadway-like theaters out of town. Now when you go to a regional theater or a place like the Manhattan Theater Club, everything is much smaller, and so it can't be exactly destined for Broadway. You can't do a big musical this way. You could not do *The Producers* at a place like the Manhattan Theater Club.

EBB: It's all so very corporate now. You don't have the independent, gutsy producers like Hal Prince anymore.

KANDER: I don't want this to sound like one of those "good old days" laments because I don't feel that way about most of life. But a great deal has changed between the conglomerates and the enormous expense of doing anything on Broadway. Today when you have a two-man show and you have an award for the producers, fifty producers walk up on the stage. I miss the easy vitality of the theater that we went into. Oddly enough, I don't think we lack talent. There's always new talent coming up. But the atmosphere has changed. It stems from the business because for investors to get their money back, a show now has to run for years at capacity in a theater that's often much too large for the material, and that's a shame. I miss the fact that Hal could write to his investors and say, "I'm doing a new show budgeted at such and such. Do you want to come in with me?" And they would support him without even knowing necessarily what it was.

EBB: Yes, even if there were no stars. Now investors look for stars. Television names. Movie names. That didn't seem to mean anything before.

KANDER: But the fact is that a show that would have cost $150,000 then now costs $8 or $9 million. I mean, millions of dollars! So when critics write about the theater and say, "What's happened? Where are all the great talents that we used to have?" the answer is, they're all over the place, but where do they get a chance to work?

EBB: It is dismaying for me to see something like *Mamma Mia* and have to wonder where is everything we've ever learned about the theater. Why has so much of that gone out the window?

KANDER: I didn't react as badly as you did to that show. I

didn't think it was all that wonderful, but I saw it as a mindless happy time for the audience.

EBB: And a million dollars gross a week. Mindless is not necessarily good. Mindless used to be *Lend an Ear* or *Touch and Go*. That kind of smart "new faces" revue. It was never this kind of empty-headed dumbness that we see so much these days.

KANDER: There was plenty of empty-headed, Freddy.

EBB: But that was all that succeeded last season. It wasn't like at the same time we had a *Guys and Dolls* or one of those.

KANDER: What is much more dismaying to me is the gigantic musical, the big spectacle. If *Mamma Mia* wants to happen, it's a modest little musical and some people adore it. I don't think it's nearly as destructive as *The Lion King*, as beautiful as those costumes are.

EBB: I actually don't think of *The Lion King* as a musical. It seems more like a Radio City Music Hall show to me, like a great big parade of costumes.

KANDER: But writers like us don't go to those—

EBB: And want to go home to write another *Lion King*. I did want to write another *Guys and Dolls*, though. And *South Pacific*. And *The King and I*. And *Forum*. I'm not inspired to want to do much of what we are seeing in the theater now. At some time in my life, I must have had the arrogance to believe that I could possibly do as well as those shows I mentioned if I kept trying and learning and working. That was my goal. *The Lion King* would never have been my goal. Nor would *Mamma Mia*. I don't get those. They go over my head, and I saw *Mamma Mia* three times.

KANDER: Why?

EBB: Because I kept looking for the virtue of it. I kept asking myself, why is this show so successful? What kind of chemistry is this?

KANDER: Freddy, that's like looking for the caviar in a peanut butter sandwich.

EBB: I feel there is something that can be learned from all successful productions. We just have to figure out what it is. Why is it happening? As far as the impact of that show, the audience was never less than ecstatic every time I went. They were jumping up and dancing. There were wild middle-aged men running down the aisles.

KANDER: It was all about their youth, Freddy.

EBB: So that may be what we come away with. I remember one show I saw recently that really impressed me as being first-rate. The Manhattan Theater Club's presentation of *The Wild Party*.

KANDER: I agree with you on that one.

EBB: I admired that piece in every way. I thought that scenery was marvelous, the direction apt, and the boy who wrote the score—

KANDER: He got killed for writing that show.

EBB: Andrew Lippa.

KANDER: Something else has happened in recent years. You can see things that are not only pieces that you admire but that are created by talented people, and the hardest thing today is to have those be accepted. We always go back to the old story of how *Flora* flopped and without hesitation Hal said, "Let's go to work on *Cabaret*."

EBB: We survived *Flora*, and Jerry and Sheldon could survive *The Body Beautiful* and go on to *Fiddler*.

KANDER: But where is Andrew's next show? That kid really has what I think of as a remarkable gift. He wasn't trying to be fashionable. His writing on that show wasn't cluttered. It wasn't overextended. It wasn't bloated. It was just talent.

EBB: The writing was so clear that I wanted to come home and be Andrew Lippa.

KANDER: *Urinetown* is not a piece that I love, but I came away thinking these people are very talented and I can't wait to see their next show. *Nine* was another score I wish that I had

written because it was done so well. I thought it was extraordinarily inventive and wonderfully melodic. At the time I hadn't
met the composer, Maury Yeston, but I think I called or wrote to
tell him his work really dazzled me. When I hear something I really respond to like that, it makes me feel like being a composer
again. It's energizing rather than depressing, as it can be. Every
once in a while something like that will happen. But I don't think
the commercial theater is set up to nurture young talent. I think
that is the most telling change that we have seen in recent years.
Our generation of writers like Steve Sondheim, Bock and Harnick, Jerry Herman—

EBB: We had the opportunity to fail.

KANDER: To be lousy.

EBB: I don't think anybody has that freedom today. The failure of that show for Andrew Lippa would seem to preclude the
possibility of his getting another one, though I hope not.

KANDER: If Andrew had written that show in 1964, he
would have already had two more shows on and had a chance to
grow. The only way you can grow is to see your work out there.
Another type of popular show that disheartens me is the "sung
through" musical. I think of it as fake opera. The *Les Miz* kind of
show. *Miss Saigon*. Sung speech is often presented simply because
it sounds artistic. But there is a difference between real opera and
fake opera. It's like pornography—you know it when you see it or
hear it. To me sung speech seems terribly pretentious and it also
deludes audiences into thinking they are having a deep experience. I hear a lot of scores, and many of them are sort of extrava-
gant takeoffs or imitations of *Les Miz* or some big gothic
production. We're in funny times in terms of what the Broadway
musical is. Much of it has to do with the perceptions of producers and theater owners as to what will sell. I went to see *Hairspray*
the other night, and I had a good time, but again it didn't make
me want to write.

EBB: I did want to write. I wanted to write and tell them to go home and listen to Frank Loesser, which would be good advice for anybody.

KANDER: But it's a huge hit, Freddy. We're in a *Hairspray* era right now. The critics adore it and the audience does too. It makes me feel a little disconnected.

EBB: There's no way for us to relate to it. It's the same sort of phenomenon as *Mamma Mia*. If you are a young writer today and you ask yourself what you have to do to succeed, those are your role models.

KANDER: Maybe in recent decades we've all taken it too seriously. In the early seventies, critics started writing about musical theater in very serious intellectual terms, sometimes suggesting that the musical was America's great gift to the theater world. In some ways I think it's unfortunate that we ever started to think that way. It used to be that shows were just entertainments. Entertainment is not a bad word. It's something Shakespeare knew very well.

EBB: I don't think many people writing today even know basically what constitutes a rhyme.

KANDER: I hope this isn't old-fogeyness setting in, but many contemporary lyrics don't rhyme not because they are intentionally not rhyming but because the people writing the lyrics don't know the difference.

EBB: They often don't hear the rhymes. Here's one of my favorites even though it's an old song—but then again, I'm an old songwriter. In "Lady of Spain," the line "I adore you" is supposed to rhyme with "first saw you." But that's not a rhyme. It's an incongruous sound, and you have to be a New Yawker to even make it work: "sore you." In terms of rhyme and prosody, our generation learned from all our predecessors, and not just Oscar Hammerstein, as brilliant as he was. I think Cole Porter's rhymes are not only ingenious, they are always correct. He is quite remarkable just from that standpoint alone.

KANDER: But with popular music, if you go back to songs

from the twenties and thirties, for the most part the grammar was correct, and for the most part the rhymes and prosody were also correct.

E B B : It may be old-fashioned, but I also find that to be true. That is how we were taught to do what we do.

K A N D E R : By tradition. It's what we grew up hearing. If you listen to "Sweet Adeline," it's a song that rhymes. The sentences are sentences. The most basic song would have had good grammar and straightforward lyrics expressed musically in such a way that you could hear them and understand them. I think that it is the change that is more remarkable than the tradition, and as far as I can tell the change happened not because people decided that they wanted to change but because of a lowering of standards in teaching English, and, of course, the music business also changed. In 1966, while I was unpacking in my hotel room in Boston, I heard "What good is sitting alone in your room . . ." on the radio. *Cabaret* hadn't even opened yet, but already the title song was a hit. I think that was probably the last year that Broadway show tunes regularly became popular hits.

It's not that great songs were no longer being written, but the music and theater worlds had changed. When popular music stopped caring about theater music, people who wrote for the theater stopped trying to write for that market. What was the point of trying to lay in a bunch of hit songs for a show if there was no one willing to record them? Rock groups figured out they could make more money if they wrote their own material rather than depending on professional songwriters. After *Cabaret*, songs from musicals ceased to be the music that the music business wanted to promote. There wasn't enough profit in it, and so little by little popular music and theater music parted ways.

E B B : I never felt overly concerned about the invasion of rock and *Hair* in that era as far as the impact of popular music on Broadway and on our careers was concerned. But I felt dismay that some executive at a record company decided that this is what the public wanted to hear, and suddenly it was mostly rock and roll and more frivolous songs that were making it. That was somewhat disheartening, but I always felt we had a fairly secure idea of what we wanted to do, and as long as we were being asked to do it, what was the problem? We were asked to do *Cabaret*, *The Happy Time*, *The Act*, *The Rink*. Those shows came to us, and so why be resentful of other musical styles? It's like the old line about another man's wife—you have to stay in your own backyard.

KANDER: I remember when "Send in the Clowns" became a pop hit, and all of us pricked up our ears, thinking that maybe things might be changing, but they weren't. It was an aberration.

EBB: They had a pop icon singing it. You can't sit down and say, We are now going to write a popular song, or a top-ten song, or even a showstopper. You can't bring that kind of goal into the writing process because it won't happen and it's a ridiculous thing to ask of yourself.

KANDER: Why try to be somebody else? What is the point of that? It often happens these days that performers attempt to change their whole presentation and musical style in order to sound more contemporary. "Contemporary" is a word that sometimes confounds me, but basically it means you're alive today. Usually, it seems to me, that kind of stylistic change doesn't work. It may be fun for an audience to hear performers stretch into some other musical form, but that is not really where they live. In our case, we can only speak our own language and write in our own style, as we always have.

EBB: And hope that someone produces us. We'll see what happens with the next one. I think we'll get on. As the French say, *Qui vivra verra*—He who lives will see.